The Small Church at Large

The Small Church at Large

Thinking Local in a Global Context

Robin J. Trebilcock

Abingdon Press
Nashville

THE SMALL CHURCH AT LARGE
THINKING LOCAL IN A GLOBAL CONTEXT

Copyright © 2003 by Robin J. Trebilcock

All rights reserved.

Scripture references unless otherwise indicated are from the *New Revised Standard Version of the Bible*, © copyright 1989 by the National Council of Churches of Christ. Used by permission.

Library of Congress Cataloging-in-Publication Data on file

Contents

Foreword   9

Prologue
  The Small Church at Large   15

The Freedom to be Open   16

At Large in the World and
  at Home With Other Christians   17

"At Large" Is Reaching Out in Local Mission   19

Chapter 1 The Small Church and Big Possibilities   27

Big On God: Re-Imaging Small Church Ministry   27

Big On Creative Energy: The Edge of Chaos   30

  Assessing the risks   31

  Countering the drive for
    administrative simplification   33

Big On Opportunity: All Things to All People and
Multiple Mission Outreach Communities   35

  Demographic "zoning" and outreach   35

  Psychosocial "zoning" and outreach   37

  Character-based "zoning" and outreach   38

  Mixed and matched for mission:
    a multi-campus church   40

10871o

Chapter 2 Thriving in a Climate of Change 43

Local Gusts and Eddies of Change 44

The Climate of Global Change 44

Local Ministry and Global Change 46

Ministry in a hostile mission field 46

Ministry in a distrustful mission field 48

Distrust of Authority 48

Distrust of Ideology 48

Distrust of Systems 49

Distrust of Motives 50

The Small Church at Large in
a Changing Mission Field 50

Undaunted by hostility 51

Spiritually literate 54

Using distrust as a tool 58

Chapter 3 Open Gates to Greener Pastures of Spirit 63

The Church is "Spirit On Offer" 64

Searching For Greener Pastures 66

Psychosocial zoning and Spirit 67

"Character" zoning and Spirit 69

Demographic zoning and Spirit 71

Open Gates to Spiritual Engagement 72

The gate that opens onto Spirit companionship 73

The gate that opens onto worship 74

The gate that opens onto Jesus 75

The gate that opens onto discipleship 77

The gate that opens onto leadership 77

Chapter 4 Network Relationships   81

Creating a Network   81

    Uncertainty   82

    Faith and uncertainty   84

Communication   86

Minimizing Control   87

Talking the Talk and Walking the Walk   90

    Situation: relating to the area   92

    Spirit: relating to faith   94

    Implementation and revision:
       relating to the task   97

Growing Leaders   102

Epilogue Thinking Local in a Global Context   109

The Place of the Sacred in the Global Village   109

    Globalization and effective local action   114

Convergence
The Mingling of Spirit and Culture in the Postmodern World

The metaphor *convergence* comes from the many "road" stories of Luke-Acts, in which again and again there is a providential convergence of human creativity, spiritual yearning, and intervening grace. These convergences are never suspended in time, but occur in the very movement and motion of everyday, fast-paced change. They are providential accidents, and therefore, from the vantage point of spiritual growth, no accidents at all. But are they human achievements? Or divine revelations? Are they a product of organizational strategic planning or metaphysical manipulation? The answer is both or neither, but it is difficult to judge from a moving vehicle.

A paradigm for contemporary experience is found in the story of Philip on the Gaza road. The spirit commands the apostle to get up and go, and he simply got up and went. No strategic planning. No social safety nets. No letters home justifying seemingly irrational behavior. Yet there is a method to this madness, revealed by the manner in which Philip joins the Ethiopian CEO in his chariot and initiates conversation in the back seat behind the chauffeur's back. It is not just that Philip can interpret the scriptures to the businessman, but that he can rely on the fact that business itself has become so spiritual that the CEO is already thinking about God. Capitalist pragmatism and spiritual urgency merge when they both spy a mud puddle and together leap to the conclusion that there is really nothing to prevent him being baptized then and now.

The spirit is poured out, but there is no resulting institutionalization of the event. No confirmation parties, no oaths of membership, no commemorative stained glass, no nominations to the official board, and no contributions to denominational generic mission funds. Instead the chariot lurches down the interstate, and organizational savvy has suddenly been harnessed by spiritual purposefulness in the interests of social service. Presumably, the Ethiopian CEO is about to enter politics, reform health care, improve the lot of the poor and oppressed, and generally innovate a way for the gospel to change a nation.

Meanwhile, Philip is again on the move. It is unclear whether the spirit miraculously transported him, or whether he cleverly purchased the plane ticket, but probably it is both. A canny reading of demographic shifts combines with a serious prayer life, and suddenly Philip pops up again in Caesarea.

That is *convergence*: the mingling of spirit and culture. The new millennium witnesses a convergence of ideas and lifestyles unknown since the first centuries of the Common Era. Not only are the old boundaries between states, economies, and cultures vanishing, but so also the boundaries between public sectors, educational disciplines, and personal lifestyles are blurring. As the old boundaries between secular and sacred disappear, a convergence of spirit and culture reveals a mingling of spirituality, organizational life, and daily living that challenges and inspires Christian leadership.

The *Convergence* ebook series offers Christian leaders insight into the confluence of ideas that are reshaping Christian mission, and coaching amid the chaotic merging of faith, lifestyle, and vocation.

Books in the series are aimed at Christian leaders within the institutional church, beyond the institutional church, and living "in between" organizational paradigms, who are interested in growing disciples and creating "discipling" communities. Whatever the topic, books in the series reflect five characteristics.

1) *Biblical grounding* in the key significance of the person and work of Jesus;

2) *Historic continuity* with the mission outreach of the earliest church;

3) *Cross-sector impact* with relevance within and beyond traditional church contexts;

4) *Lifestyle coaching* that emphasizes holistic living and practical application to diverse experience;

5) *Non-ecclesiastical perspective* that avoids traditional church terminology, institutional polity disputes, and dichotomies between clergy and laity, and focuses on teams, core values, and volunteer empowerment.

The *Convergence* Book series provides Christian leaders with significant reading that does not "fit" into any of the traditional niche publishing of old modernity. These are books that leaders in any and all disciplines may desperately desire to dismiss as shallow or impossible, but that must inescapably be taken seriously. They represent the cutting edge and the seamless synthesis that *is* the postmodern world.

Welcome to Robin Trebilcock's Mission Field

This book is about what happens when small churches discover ancient mission in the contemporary world. Prospect Road Uniting Church is a ministry composed of five little churches in Adelaide, Australia. Robin came to these five declining, defensive, small churches in 1996. Today there are still five churches. They are still small. But they are no longer five timid congregations clinging to survival, but five centers of indigenous mission spanning the micro-cultures of urban Adelaide and the Australian outback.

Australia is further than even Europe or Canada into the postmodern, multi-cultural, contemporary world that is a ferment of spirituality in which Christianity is but a small potato. The United

States is even further behind, but all these countries are catching up fast. With over 80 percent of the churches in North America worshipping less than 100 people, and most of them struggling to keep their clergy, balance the budget, and just survive, a success story from Australia should come as welcome news.

Or perhaps not. Robin is about to describe a church transformation that has come at significant cost. There is hope for the small church, but only if the small church surrenders organizational models, worship patterns, stewardship assumptions, leadership expectations, and minority self-interest that has come to be more precious to small churches than the gospel itself. The competition that challenges the future of the small church is not the influence of other major religions; nor is it the influence of deified cultural forms of sports, success, profit, or politics. The real competition comes from within the small church itself. It is the smallness of its vision, the smallness of its inclusivity, and the smallness of its heart. Robin proves that neither the lack nor the abundance of resources will be decisive for the future of the small church. Imagination, sensitivity, leadership, and sheer undiluted faithfulness will win out every time.

One of the most important things you need to know about Robin is that he is definitely *not* the kind of leader so many struggling small churches dream about. He is not young, charismatic, extroverted, or hyper-kinetic. He is anticipating carrying on mission in retirement, reflective, introverted, and careful. One doubts that he will magnetically attract the youth or constantly visit the elderly. He has no grand ideas to grow a mega-church on the prairie or in the urban core, nor does he waste time inventing fundraisers to keep the heating bills paid and the doors open. In short, many small churches in North America might well overlook his cultural insight and leadership potential—and indeed, in my experience as a consultant, that is precisely what many small churches do when looking for the right pastor.

Robin's gifts are of a different kind, and you will see them peek out of the corners of this book through provocative insights, off-hand comments, and suddenly significant connections between ideas and cultures and histories. Here are my top four favorite insights in the book you are about to read.

12

First, Robin will introduce you to a whole new idea of "shepherding." Learning from contemporary sheep ranching strategies from a land with little water, he will introduce you to an "open range" philosophy of shepherding that has nothing to do with guiding sheep and everything to do with letting them roam where they will.

Second, Robin will introduce you to a different kind of leadership. Forced to provide spiritual guidance to people over a huge geographical area, spanning multiple micro-cultures, he will describe a new metaphor of ministry by "walk-around." Never get tied down by a handful of needy parishioners demanding to be "taken care of"; constantly move among non-church members to learn how to satisfy their unique hunger with the gospel; intervene to coach church leaders whenever possible; and trust other leaders to invent their own programs.

Third, Robin will prove to you that even small churches with limited resources can provide multiple-option ministries to the diverse public. One size no longer fits all. Five little churches can design five totally distinctive missions aimed at very different cultures—and still share the same spiritual identity, mission purpose, and pastoral leadership. The days are over for the circuit rider wearing himself or herself out preaching the same sermon, implementing the same liturgy, and repeating the same things from preaching point to preaching point.

Finally, Robin will demonstrate the power of micro-macro connections. Mere ministry to the region or the neighborhood will never capture the imagination of the postmodern, highly mobile, internet connected public. Their respect is given only to those organizations that can connect local experience with global relationships. Robin has an ability to translate global trends into local mission opportunities, and as you will see he has the ability to carry ordinary people beyond their local environment to have impact upon the world. Here is a new fusion of evangelism and social action in the small church that connects the neighborhood with the neighboring country.

As I read Robin's manuscript, e-mailed in stages from Australia, my heart constantly drifted to two kinds of churches. I hope the people in these two kinds of churches—or the people who identify with these kind of churches—will take the lessons of this book to heart.

My heart leapt for the "outport" churches of Newfoundland. I consulted among those churches, and coached their leaders, and these lessons from Australia can help their mission. Small, isolated clusters of churches, with limited resources, yet with deep faith and outgoing spirits; these "outports" can thrive as the body of Christ if the leaders can capture a new vision of ministry.

My heart also leapt for the "urban core" churches of Miami, New York, Los Angeles, and so many other cities. Many are non-Caucasian. English is not their first language, and western European culture is more foe than friend. They often feel misunderstood by denominations, and ignored by seminaries. Yet they can thrive as the body of Christ if their members can imagine a different way to be the church.

Small is not beautiful. Big is not beautiful. Size and resource have nothing to do with the real beauty of a church. The beauty of a church lies in its willingness to learn from any source, and adapt in any way, to connect with every culture, so that as many people as possible can experience Jesus Christ.

Tom Bandy and Bill Easum, *General Editors*

THE SMALL CHURCH AT LARGE

There is a different feel now to Prospect Road Uniting Church in Adelaide, Australia, that was not present when I began my pastoral ministry in 1996. Then it was a fairly typical cluster of five small congregations, served for essentially economic reasons by a single staff person. I rotated around worship that was uniformly traditional and mostly at the same time on Sunday morning in every centre. Prospect Road is still a cluster of five centres with a single pastor, but that is where the similarity ends. Now each centre has a special role in the overall outreach of the church. Each has a different style and time of worship. Each has turned from having a stoic determination to survive into having a joyous Christian expectation of life. Prospect Road has an open style, an open relationship to its mission target groups, an open administrative structure, an open acceptance of the changes in global society, and an open and deepening relationship to God. It is a church "at large."

Some years ago in another cluster of small rural churches, our church secretary (chair of the board) was a very progressive sheep farmer (a "pastoralist," in our culture) named Robert. Robert developed innovative farm management practices that allowed him to thrive rather than survive in the worst seasons on the semi-arid pastureland of his farm. Something of what Robert did carried over into the change and transformation of Prospect Road— change and transformation that has allowed it to thrive through the "hard seasons" that most local churches are facing today throughout the globe.

Robert's innovations gave the sheep the freedom to manage their own future. In times of drought, sheep stay very close to water. Consequently they eat all the grass close to the water until they reach the point where the available grass is too far away from the water—and then they starve. Robert overcame this with a series of radical moves. He deliberately under-grazed his pasture. He reticulated water to every part of his large property. In time of drought, he reduced his flock to breeding ewes, opened every gate, and allowed his sheep to spread out over the whole of the property. His sheep not only survived, they actually thrived in the harsh conditions.

An open church is like Robert's place. In an open church there is ready access to "living water" and "spiritual food" no matter where a person may be in his or her spiritual journey. The gates are open.

THE FREEDOM TO BE OPEN

The small church functions as a mission outpost in an increasingly hostile world. Huston Smith, in *Why Religion Matters—The Fate of the Human Spirit in an Age of Disbelief* [1] examines the way that the scientific rationalism of the modern era has nurtured a worldview that is hostile to religion. In Australia, this hostility toward religion is endemic, finding fertile ground in an anti-authoritarian, anti-organized character trait. This attitude stems in part from the attitudes of early Australia as a penal colony and as a destination for economic refugees from Britain and Europe. Other parts of the globe, especially those with new immigrant populations, are experiencing similar hostility, or at best, indifference. It is a tough time to be a small church and the setting is getting tougher.

In a hostile climate there is a natural tendency toward defensive, conservative values. This response is a capitulation to the difficulties. The pioneer wagons in the defensive circle against the marauding tribes are stuck; even though within the circle there will be feelings of normalcy and safety. The church at large is a church moving forward in freedom through its knowledge of the terrain and the ways of the world in which it is traveling and a vision of the new land to which it is headed.

The small church is especially prone to a defensive reaction to its situation because it is small. The megachurch is the paradigm of the successful church in our time. It seems like a no-win situation to compare a church with a single pastor and a small bunch of senior citizens with the resources of membership, staff, and budget of the most successful churches. But small churches like Prospect Road that work and witness "at large" in their local areas can be effective and lively, and will grow numerically and spiritually. The small church at large is free from fear of the future and released from any sense of inadequacy. God blesses the gifts of the small church that are offered in sincerity, faith, and trust.

The bureaucratic model of a church entrenched in denominational structures often works against allowing the small church to be at large. The big churches do not need denominational structures and can ignore them with a degree of impunity, but not small churches. Being *at large* as a small church requires subtlety, astuteness, and avoidance of control in relating to denominational authorities. Local, indigenous knowledge and mission experimentation will be more effective than blanket theories from afar. Funding submissions, in particular, need to work in the local scene and be "adjusted" to suit bureaucratic requirements, rather than the other way around.

The ability of small churches to be at large can be restricted by leadership whose skills and status are vested in maintaining a defensive circle against a hostile world. In a small church such leadership can manipulate the fear of losing people and shrinking and weakening the church. In our times, any forms of authoritarianism work against newcomers being attracted to the church, thus triggering a cycle of decline. Astute, informed, and strong leadership must win over the middle ground of a small church's constituency in order to create the spirit of innovation, openness, and change that will allow it to be "at large."

AT LARGE IN THE WORLD AND AT HOME WITH OTHER CHRISTIANS

Christendom is defined as *Church* in the modern era, which is now passing. In Christendom, belonging to a church had an element of possessiveness built into it. Churches in that era felt that they were in a Christian world where most of the people were willing to belong to a church. The question was, "Which one?" Churches were concerned with market share. Other churches were the competition—potential "sheep stealers" of those who belonged to a particular church's flock. Open community avoids competition between churches. In the past, our five little congregations lost a lot of energy looking over their shoulders to see if one of the others was getting more of the "available" resources, or more of the pastor's time. The Anglicans and the Baptists down the road were a threat. These attitudes were in denial of the reality of the situation they were in. In looking at the limited number of "churchgoers" waiting to be recruited to Prospect Road, they were blind to the large numbers of "non-churchgoers." There are 30,000 people on our patch. If we filled up every available pew in every church we might account for 5,000 people. We are in a mission field. We are in competition with the principalities and powers[2] of this world, not other Christians. On Robert's farm, the sheep did not have to compete with one another for the grass and water; they had to overcome the drought conditions. So if another church wins someone for Christ, then praise God and learn from its success. In our times there are plenty of new people to be won.

A Greek Pentecostal evangelist, Peter Kahrimanis, came to us at Prospect Road, asking for permission to work from one of our centres. Neither "mainstream" nor in ecumenical relationship nor even properly accredited, under the old attitudes he would have been seen as "alien" and someone who was out to subvert and "capture" our people for his own fellowship. We acceded to his request. Being open and a church "at large" means that people are trusted to choose and decide their Christian journey. If with Peter? Praise the Lord! If with Prospect Road? Praise the Lord too. If, as it turned out, with both, then what a rich faith journey they are experiencing. Our experience with Peter has been mutually enriching. We would never have reached the people on the margins that he is reaching. Each of us is learning new insights into ministry by working with the other. We are learning hospitality evangelism, and insights into the symbolic value of "prosperity" in ministry to needy people, from Peter. In turn, this leader is learning how to be more comprehensive in his approach to mission and to develop a structural relationship with "mainstream" transformational church life. In contrast, one of the churches "down the road" is mainstream, in ecumenical relationship with us, and with accredited leadership. But when we tried to network our young parents' program with theirs, our correspondence was discarded and discounted, because we were "opposition." Like Jesus, we asked the question, "Which of these . . . , do you think, was a neighbor?"[3] and we discerned the same answer as that given so long ago—"The one who showed . . . mercy." Jesus said, "Go and do likewise."

Such openness has not been easy to maintain or digest. There are few of the comforting similarities that make this "sister church" relationship. The main criterion is "Does this ministry bring people to Jesus?" to which we added, "Does this ministry bring *different* people to Jesus than our ministry?" With a "Yes!" to both, all the other questions can be worked through—and there are many! The most potentially disturbing is the question of "proprietary rights." The paradox is to care deeply as responsible stewards, while at the same time risking property use by people who have less care. Another paradox is that the pastor and the church have to live with both "Everything is important" and "Nothing is important." That is, pastor and church need to be absolutely clear about their own core values, bedrock beliefs, and motivating vision because a mission partner has different values, beliefs, and vision That gap creates uncertainty, an "edge of chaos" challenge to harmony, and the potential for friction. "Regard everything as loss because of the surpassing value of knowing Christ Jesus my Lord," Paul says in Philippians 3:8, reflecting on the paradox of his Jewish orthodoxy and his Gentile mission. A similar generosity of spirit is needed to make mission partnerships work.

"AT LARGE" IS REACHING OUT IN LOCAL MISSION

In the Christendom from which we are now emerging, almost everyone in a Christian country belonged to a church. So mission was focused on foreign countries where people were not Christian. Mission became separated from the local context and became the provenance of a few unique and hardy individuals who faced extraordinary challenges to bring the gospel to people who had never heard it. Today the mission field is down the street from the church, around the corner from where we live, and over the back fence.

When mission was somewhere else, the Church concentrated on nurturing those who belonged—acculturating, teaching, making a relationship with Jesus an explicit and sometimes intense experience and keeping people enfolded, mostly into the flock into which they had been born. The Church turned in on itself, concentrating on maintaining what it had. Today churches face a choice of nurturing fewer and fewer people or going out as missionaries into their local mission field. The local church has to turn itself inside out and focus on the people beyond it. Being "at large" means reaching out in local mission.

Jesus himself demonstrated this to his home congregation at Nazareth—and experienced the ire of people locked into having their own needs satisfied. Jesus reminded them of how God is "at large" in ministering to people's needs, feeding the foreign widow in the drought, and healing the foreign general. Jesus preached this as a proclamation of his own decision to be "at large" in his ministry and mission.[4]

When Jesus had gathered a group of disciples and followers, he did not allow them to become privileged "insiders" but sent them out to be "at large," to engage in local mission—first the twelve disciples and then seventy of his followers. That must have been a high proportion of the followers he had. Jesus himself remarks, "The harvest is plentiful, but the laborers are few." In his training session, Jesus told them to go out to bring peace to households, cure the sick, proclaim the Kingdom, and accept hospitality. Those were the ministries that raised the issue of Spirit in Jesus' day. The seventy followers showed people how to be fulfilled in their Spirit-led searches. In our day, the searches will be different and the offer of Spirit framed in a different context, but the need for the small, local church to train and equip its followers to be local missionaries is no less urgent.

We could look to the pioneers of our own Church tradition to find further examples of people who responded to Jesus' presence in a changing world and worked outside a church that they saw was trying to ignore and resist the changes and were therefore not with Jesus in mission. We have forgotten that the great confessions of faith that are clung to now were once radical calls for faith to emerge from the ignorance and superstition that was prevalent in those times. The Reformers moved outside the Church to create new civic and national identities based on knowledge of Jesus obtained at first hand, through scriptures and texts made available to all in everyday language. The Wesleys and the revivalists moved outside the Church to touch and win people who were there for Jesus—again, they looked *outside* the Church.

My particular hero is not from my tradition. He inspires me because of his radical response to a rationalist worldview that was hostile to the Church—a situation that all churches face today. In the middle of the nineteenth century a young Catholic priest, Jules Chevalier, was posted to a town in central France that had become a hotbed of the anti-religious, anti-clerical rationalism that swept France after the Revolution. He transformed that local church, against incredible opposition, by promoting missionary values. He rebuilt relationships between people and the church by rebuilding relationships between people and Jesus. He discerned and pioneered a new way of being Church that touched the spiritual needs of people whose relationships had been wounded by the Revolution, the bloody political and social upheaval that followed, and the Napoleonic Wars. In the process of doing this, he founded a new religious order, the Missionaries of the Sacred Heart.[5]

Jules Chevalier found a way to remain "orthodox" in the Catholic tradition without being the "pre-modern" Church that had been so soundly rejected by the people. The most obvious response to the new worldview on the mission field—developing a "rational" faith was denied to him because it was so strongly identified with Protestantism. Instead he transformed the traditional Catholic piety about the Sacred Heart of Jesus from a mystical piety to an affective, relational piety. He developed a new image and role for Mary that helped people to relate to Jesus and God and be sustained in patience, courage, and hope for the future through a time of French/European history of great political and social upheaval. His "transitioned" church and religious order became a popular movement and the little town became a center of pilgrimage. It did so without apparitions or miracles—in that sense the movement was rational—but it was the sense of relationship with Church, Mary, Jesus, and God (and the compassion of God, Jesus, Mary and Church toward them in their difficulty) that turned around personal faith. There is much more to say about Chevalier's handling of persecution by the government and the order's role as pioneering missionaries in northern Australia and the Pacific islands, but it is his sense and style of transforming the Church to minister in a hostile mission field that makes Jules Chevalier my hero and his work relevant for any church trying to evangelize today's hostile mission field and its scientific rationalism.

We are blessed in our time by Christian authors and consultants who are wrestling with the issues facing Christian faith today and offering ways for the Church to be "at large." Prospect Road and I have been helped particularly by two transformational leaders, William Easum (a Texan) and Thomas Bandy (a Canadian) and the relational network of pastors and church leaders around the globe they have built through their website, books, seminars and on-line coaching. They, and others like them, help us to engage with an increasingly hostile mission field with courage, effective methodologies, and a transforming hope for the future. As in first-century Judea, sixteenth-century Europe and nineteenth-century France, some twenty-first century churches are finding new ways of being Church that make them effective mission outposts in their districts.

So the Church in our time needs to make a radical change of focus—from nurturing to evangelizing; from waiting for people to come to it to finding the people who are waiting for it to come to them; from statements like "Jesus is the answer!" to discerning the ways and means that would introduce people to Jesus in their personal context. The Church needs to identify in its area the questions that people have about life for which Jesus is the answer. The small church at large is a church facing outward to its local mission field, not inward to the people it has. It is hard to forego their rights, entitlements, and privileges for people who are not even Christian, but no one outside the Church will become Christian until they do. A small church that has not made this turn will struggle on, wondering why people do not support such a warm and friendly bunch of people, or our denomination, or endorse our doctrines. It is because they turned inward to their own spiritual interests and became oblivious to anyone else's. Such a turnaround is not easily accomplished. It takes courageous and visionary leadership

Leadership At Large

The small church at large needs leadership at large. By returning to our farm metaphor, every day Robert would drive around the property, checking the sheep and their feed and water and making sure their infrastructure was OK. He looked out for and dealt with any stress in the flock as a whole and devised a remedy. He dealt with individual sheep in serious trouble. In my ministry at Prospect Road, I have picked up on the maxim of "management by wandering about". I keep an eye, not only on the big picture and the infrastructure but also on the spiritual condition of those receiving ministry, picking up and dealing with any major issues in individuals or the organization. There are fewer and fewer grumbles and rumbles. Personal yearning for community seems to be being met without a sense of individuals or the pastor being controlled.

It was the well-known management writer, Tom Peters, who first coined the phrase "management by wandering" around in one of his earlier books. In *Thriving on Chaos—Handbook for a Management Revolution* he returns to it again. He describes it as a way senior management, by being at the interface between the organization and its marketplace, can get a feel for the way their business's products and processes have an impact on their customers and employees. By "wandering around" the office, factory, and loading docks (and by visiting and talking with customers), faults, difficulties, and grumbles can be recognized and acted upon to improve business outcomes and profits. It gives a more accurate "big picture" of the relationship between a business and its customers as well as identifying ways that processes can be improved and workers cared for. In addition, as

Peters says:

> "To enable all organization members to get comfortable with change and constant risk-taking, management must be ever present, training, coaching, cajoling—and caring and comforting."[6]

When church leaders, and particularly pastors, are "at large" individuals receive better pastoral care because needs and responses to needs can be assessed from a broad perspective. Congregation behaviors that are petty and trivial show up. A real picture of the relationship of the church to its neighborhood and district can be discerned. The kind of Spirit the church offers to enquirers can be evaluated. Many of the aspects of church life that strengthened faith in the modern era are counter-productive now that this era is on the wane. In a rapidly changing mission field, Peters' words on management style are important for a pastor aiming to lead his or her church into effective mission outreach.

The church leader needs to be like the modern farmer. Robert changed the way he managed his farm. He deliberately understocked so the drought-resistant and highly nutritious native grasses could regenerate. He controlled feral rabbits. He fenced and sowed sand dunes with grass to stop sand drift. Once he took me out to the back of the farm. There was feed on his side of the fence and bare earth on his neighbor's side. Robert was ahead of his time. Farmers today know that the old farming methods denuded the countryside, impoverished soils, created erosion, and increased salinity. They now have to be holistic and practice sustainable farming. Churches and pastors trying to maintain church life as it was in the glory days will experience decline and difficulty unless they practice ministry that is "at large" indigenous to their area, holistic and sustainable.

Peters also talks about the symbolic role of management. By breaking down the barriers between staff, workers, and clients, a manager models behavior that encourages communication, networking, and cooperation.[7] He or she is a symbol of the company itself in its relationship to its staff, suppliers, and customers. A pastor who leads from an office deep in the bowels of church property, or from the study at home, does not model a leader "at large." Increasingly at Prospect Road, I have my office in the car and meet and talk with people in cafés over some good coffee. I meet people where they are, but this is not the role of a personal chaplain, who offends insiders if not visiting each member at home at least twice a year. It is engaging with people out in their personal mission field and supporting their outreach. I have a grid-map of cafés around my city, Adelaide, that serve good coffee, so I can arrange to meet people near where they work as well as near the church or where they live. Of course, the café in the center of my patch gets most of my "office" trade. People see me "at large" sometimes heads down over plans and papers, sometimes listening, sometimes just enjoying someone's company. They see me with lots of different people. The regular clients of the café wave or chat as they pass. Like Peters' manager, a leader "at large" is a symbol of the church in its relationship to church people, its neighborhood, and the people it seeks to serve. But a church leader is more than that. She or he is a symbol of God, incarnate in Jesus, making the coffee shop encounter a non-ritual form of communion in which the people present share the experience of the presence of Christ.

Looking back, and comparing how Prospect Road Uniting Church was and how it is now, it seems almost ludicrous that we could imagine any church thriving under that old regime. The memory and optimism of the boom days immediately after World War II blinded people to the need to do something about the decline, the retreat, and the enclosure that was taking place. There are many places where the Church is still blindly ministering in a way that it once did well but now does with a barely concealed sense of futility. All over the world there are these same little clusters of churches supporting a single pastor and more or less surviving. Now is the time for their release and transformation.

---

[1] Houston Smith, *Why Religion Matters: The Fate Of the Human Spirit In An Age Of Disbelief* (San Francisco: HarperSanFrancisco, 2001).

[2] For a broad treatment at depth of the remarks in this book, see Walter

Wink, *Engaging the Powers: Discernment and Resistance in a World of Domination* (Minneapolis: Augsburg Fortress, 1992).

[3] Luke: 10:36, 37, NRSV altered.

[4] Luke 4:16ff.

[5] E.J. Cuskelly MSC, *Jules Chevalier: Man with a Mission* (Rome: Missionaries of the Sacred Heart, 1975).

[6] Tom Peters, *Thriving on Chaos: Handbook for a Management Revolution* (London: Macmillan, 1988), p. 422ff.

[7] Tom Peters, p. 417ff.

CHAPTER 1

The Small Church & Big Possibilities

It was late afternoon and I was lying on a picnic blanket in a grassy glade in the Bunya Mountains, surrounded by the Bunya Pine trees that are unique to the area. A shaft of sunlight pierced the dark green foliage and shone into the glade. As I looked at it, I saw a veritable soup of flying insects in the air lit up by the shaft of light—mosquitoes, gnats, midges, flies, bees, dragonflies, moths, and butterflies—a yellow sea teeming with life. It was a theophany for me—a glimpse of the fullness of God, an insight into the heart of the God of plenty. I felt small in the face of such abundance, and loved too. How well God provides for creatures that we would swat without a thought! How well we are loved too!

BIG ON GOD:
RE-IMAGING SMALL CHURCH MINISTRY

Smallness daunts. In a world where all the models of success are big and all the images of progress are those of growing and expanding, being leaders and pastors of a cluster of small, declining churches can seem short on possibility. A significant small church ministry in the face of negative perceptions, little support or understanding from denominational authorities, or even from one's peers, needs a spirituality that goes beyond the "soup" of smallness and sometimes pettiness, and

- Honors God
- Seeks God's encouragement
- Discerns God's purpose and power.

The words God spoke to St. Paul are worth pondering. They can help leaders to contextualize their role in a small church, to love the mission field that God has given them, and to bring vigor to their task of evangelizing it.

> "My grace is sufficient for you, for power is made perfect in weakness."

Whether or not we need to be as vehement as he was, we need to assert the power of God as strongly in ourselves as he did to be released from the demoralizing effect of smallness.

> "So, I will boast all the more gladly of my weaknesses, so that the power of Christ may dwell in me. Therefore I am content with weaknesses, insults, hardships, persecutions, and calamities for the sake of Christ; for whenever I am weak, then I am strong."
>
> (2 Cor. 12: 9-10)

Without a strong sense of the power of God at work in the situation, it is easy for small to get smaller. In this downsizing spiral, instead of discerning what God wants in the situation, it is viewed as, "What needs to be done to keep things going?" then down another notch to, "What can be done in the circumstances?" then answered, "Not much!"

Small church leaders may not face physical danger like St. Paul, but there can be many setbacks and disappointments. Churches decline almost imperceptibly over many years. In Australia there was a noticeable collapse in the late 1960s and then life carried on more or less as usual. But then one year the basketball team folded. Another year, the Sunday school closed. The leadership stayed the same—just got older. Pastors came and left with varying degrees of effectiveness. Some were "awake" to what was happening but unable to generate enough enthusiasm to change. Australians have an expression for this. It's, "She'll be right, mate!"—a bit like the more universal, "No worries!" But everything was not alright and there should have been worries.

My church invited a farmer from one of our denomination's rural churches to speak at our annual Harvest Thanksgiving Service. We are an inner urban church. Our home gardens are no longer a basic source of the food on our table and we wanted to get in touch with and give thanks for the farmers who do put the food on our table. We had also heard that changes in global agricultural markets and other social changes had put farmers and their communities under great stress. And so it proved to be. Our visitor shared his stories of farm amalgamations, crop diversification, and more ecologically sensitive land management to redress past abuses. We learned about all the things that successful farmers needed to do to conserve the land for the future, and how different farming is today from the simple romantic images of hard work and basic tasks that we had grown up with. Now farmers must be highly knowledgeable and competent agricultural scientists, technologists, chemists, and agronomists to survive into the future.

Prospect Road's decision to be a small church that is big on change was of as much interest to our visitor as his experience of changing farming practices had been to us. The church where our farmer came from had not changed. One of a string of small centres strung out along the main road and railway line, it offered much the same as it had fifty years ago, except perhaps a change from hymns to choruses. The church turned off our visitor's sons, the new breed of farmers, just as the same age group is turned off in the city. When it comes to change and the Church, there is no city/country divide. All churches face change, and unless they respond to it, they face drastic decline and problematic survival.

Prospect Road is one of many churches throughout the world that are clusters of small, aging congregations facing an uncertain future. Global economic pressures are changing the face and viability of communities. Global changes in people's attitude towards institutions like the Church are bringing difficulties in outreach, mission, and growth. All churches are confronted by the changes of our times, but small churches feel more exposed. Prospect Road has responded in a particular way to its situation. Other churches need to consider their different settings and circumstances, in order to respond effectively to the issues of mission and praxis so that they face and grasp and grow their future possibilities. But the fundamental step of spiritual discernment is an essential beginning point. Without the spirit-lifting power of God, the task is too daunting.

BIG ON CREATIVE ENERGY: THE EDGE OF CHAOS

Prospect Road Uniting Church had to change or die. What could we do that would allow us to thrive? I had read a book on complexity and had been "playing" with the idea of linking "edge of chaos" with church growth. Could we use the "edge of chaos" hypothesis to end up as a "fitter" church? After a lot of thought, some trial and error (mostly error) at a previous church, and an intuitive leap of faith, I took Prospect Road to the edge of chaos.

The book that I had read described a number of aspects of complexity, but it was the chapter describing characteristics of the Edge of Chaos that had aroused my interest.[8] In experiments modeling a complex dynamic system of elements, using a computer, observations were made of the effect on the system of the number of connections elements had to one another. With one connection, the system remained static. With four or more connections, the network became chaotic. With two or three connections, the system evolved to a high level of "fitness." This, unexpected, intermediate zone between stability and chaos was labeled the "edge of chaos". Further work suggested that a system at the "edge of chaos" transitions into a state of high energy, adaptability, and creativity. That is what I wanted for Prospect Road.

So, we changed our existing five small declining congregations at Prospect Road to one congregation and began to transition them into four distinct outreach communities with five centres in the one church.[9] We hoped that this would generate an "edge of chaos" situation—somewhere between "no change" and "overwhelming change." Two communities seemed too few, with an increased danger of polarizing the church. Five seemed too many. Four seemed a number that would generate the "edge of chaos" stew of innovation we needed. Experience has proven this hunch. Developing the new communities has broken open the status quo, rendered the formerly deeply entrenched control mechanisms ineffective and obsolete, and opened new avenues for creativity and imagination.

We spent a lot of praying and planning time as a church. It is one thing for a pastor to take a leap of faith to use something out of a book to change the church. It is another thing for the church to decide that it should act in that way. That is where Jesus came into the picture. It was Christ and the Holy Spirit who guided us through those months before the decision was made. Jesus is an active partner in bringing a church to the edge of chaos so that it can realize its desire for change and transition.

In John 5:1-9, there is a story on the edge of chaos involving Jesus.

> After this there was a festival of the Jews, and Jesus went up to Jerusalem. Now in Jerusalem by the Sheep Gate there is a pool, called in Hebrew Beth-zatha, which has five porticoes. In these lay many invalids—blind, lame, and paralyzed. One man was there who had been ill for thirty-eight years.
>
> When Jesus saw him lying there and knew that he had been there a long time, he said to him, "Do you want to be made well?"
>
> The sick man answered him, "Sir, I have no one to put me into the pool when the water is stirred up; and while I am making my way, someone else steps down ahead of me."
>
> Jesus said to him, "Stand up, take your mat and walk."
>
> At once the man was made well, and he took up his mat and began to walk.

The ruffling of the waters by an angel is a metaphor for the edge of chaos. The man knew he would change if he could get into the edge of chaos state, but he would never have made it nor changed unless Jesus had come to be "edge of chaos" for him. And that is how it worked for us. We said "Yes!" to a system that optimized the situation we were in to be rich with future possibility and we said "Yes!" to Jesus' invitation to be rich with future possibility in him.

Assessing the risks

The very nature of the edge of chaos implies that if there is too much complexity then chaos will take over. Unfortunately, unlike computer experiments, increments of complexity in church relationships are not easy to define. Nevertheless, some risk assessment needs to be made in order to identify situations that may increase the complexity beyond the critical point. The initial choice of how many connections is the first risk. If there are too many connections to begin with, chaos will happen. That is what happened in my previous church where I first experimented with the edge of chaos. We began with five outreach communities. Three or four is safer.

There is a risk of chaos occurring if there are not clear, direct, and open opportunities to influence outreach community decisions. The previous church's leadership had too little influence in two of its five outreach communities. One of them was associated with a prestigious boy's school with historic links to the church. The church leadership had very little influence over that relationship. Another was a residential Aged Care facility adjacent to the church and with historic links to the church. There was a management link, but very little influence over the formidable gossip network such places generate. It was not just a matter of being excluded from the "line of control" in the case of the school or the network of gossip in the other. Influence, unlike control, depends on establishing mutually rewarding relationships and growing mutual respect. In both cases, not enough was done to develop these informal "influence" relationships. Too much reliance was put on the formal "control" relationships in which we were very minor players!

Leadership influence takes time to develop. When a leader is confronted by a church in serious decline, in a mission field full of possibility, the sense of urgency about the task can push the situation too far too soon. Task subsumes relationships. Pressure builds, leading to under-prepared courses of action, each "near-miss" contributing to the stress until something gives. Then chaos happens! At Prospect Road, we needed seven months of fortnightly meetings alternating between planning and prayer before people were able to discern a way forward. The leadership influence grows as everyone's relationship to God, Jesus, and the call to serve grows.

Countering the drive for administrative simplification

Going to the edge of chaos is counter-intuitive to Christendom and the modernist Church, particularly denominational authorities. Their preferred changes are toward simplification—sell, merge, and consolidate. There are three major reasons for this:

• Conforming to a standard that was effective in Christendom,
• Change in the ratios of church sites and population
• Rationalization.

When the modern epoch began, the emerging pattern of Church was anti-establishment and often illicit. When the new churches eventually became the establishment, order and stability became dominant values, and the ideal, modern Church form emerged (in its basic form) with the single pastor, single congregation, line management, a departmental structure with committees, and entitled membership. Multi-centre, shared pastor churches aspired to this structure and successful larger churches grew from such a structure. When Christendom was growing, it was a good model. Now that Christendom is shrinking, it has become a fallback model. Wherever decline happens, denominational authorities will try to find a way to consolidate to the ideal modern Church form.

Initially, the modern Church grew as pioneers in new areas. People saw "Church" as important and integral to local neighborhood infrastructure. So they took initiative, gave sacrificially, and planted churches in every green-fields housing development. The boom after World War II overwhelmed this model of church planting, and denominational authorities took on a central planning role. They related churches to demographics, working on a formula of how many denominational supporters would be available to fill each new church. As Christendom declined, so the ratios changed and new churches were more sparsely located. When denominational authorities, working on current ratios, look at the number of churches in the older neighborhoods, they want to reduce the number of churches to fit the new ratios. This is a strategy of retreat and defeat. In the area served by Prospect Road, the number of seats available in all the churches of every denomination is only twenty percent of the population and those seats are only half filled. There is no lack of people on the mission field. The problem is not redundancy but potency! This retreat is masked by an illusion of moving forward by the construction of new buildings. Every new building gives a sense of accomplishment and pride in the denomination (and its authorities) that masks the number of churches in survival mode or that are "disappeared" by being amalgamated.

Rationalization is one of the most socially destructive strategies of the late modernist epoch. Its goal is maximizing money, not maximizing mission, although "releasing funds for mission" is often quoted as justification for rationalization. Like the planning criteria, rationalization avoids the hard work of engaging in mission by suggesting that newer and bigger will attract attendance. But unless outreach methods and attitudes change, mission ineffectiveness will prevail. When two or three little heaps of ineffectiveness are piled together, what results is a bigger heap of ineffectiveness. Somewhere, the question of effectiveness has to be faced. Why not with pre-rationalized small churches? Economics are usually at the center of rationalized moves. At Prospect Road we calculated differently. The multiple local overheads may be rationally inefficient but easily covered by local financial support. If we sold up and relocated, we would incur a substantial debt, lose much of the local support, lose more than 50 percent of our seating capacity, and have about 80 percent less space and less flexibility about how to use it. We lose connection with the neighborhood and accessibility is reduced. Two small church clusters in Adelaide which have recently tried to amalgamate have lost attendees and mission momentum through stalled action and internal acrimony that will take years to recover. When the social issues are considered as well as the money, rationalization is less attractive. There will be some situations where a centre is redundant, but mission effectiveness must be the first and major consideration. Unless modernist, Christendom churches change to be effective in their outreach, they will remain a liability rather than an asset for Jesus, no matter what local or denominational authorities propose.

BIG ON OPPORTUNITY: ALL THINGS TO ALL PEOPLE AND MULTIPLE MISSION OUTREACH COMMUNITIES

We decided we needed four outreach communities at Prospect Road to get into the "edge of chaos" zone. How would we choose which four? We decided to look at who inhabited our mission field and try to choose our communities so that each could identify with some of those people and together we might appeal to them all. Like Paul, we resolved to be all things to all people, that we by all means save some.

> For though I am free with respect to all, I have made myself a slave to all, so that I might win more of them. To the Jews I became as a Jew, in order to win Jews. To those under the law I became as one under the law (though I myself am not under the law) so that I might win those under the law. To those outside the law I became as one outside the law (though I am not free from God's law but am under Christ's law) so that I might win those outside the law. To the weak I became weak, so that I might win the weak. I have become all things to all people, that I might by all means save some. 1 Corinthians 9:19-22

St. Paul would have had an outreach community for slaves, one for Jews, one for Gentiles, and one for the weak. We chose three different screens to show us the people on whom we should focus our ministry. We were looking for four groups. Initially we found three. We could have run with three and still been in the "edge of chaos" zone, but we refined our search and subdivided the major group into two. So we had the four we were looking for. The groups were chosen on the basis of three different sets of data—demography, a psychosocial profile, and consideration of character.

Demographic "zoning" and outreach

Our first criterion was demography. Our patch has three major demographic groupings. Prospect Road Uniting Church serves a mostly residential suburban area that is in the first ring from the Central Business District of Adelaide. In the center of the patch are young Gen-X professionals buying and renovating old homes and raising families. This seemed to identify one mission focus. Nearer the CBD are alternative lifestyle people—creative people with an interest in social issues—more singles and DINK (dual-income with no kids) Gen-Xers. This was a different mission focus. Farthest out, there is an area of low-income housing. This identified a third mission focus. So, at Prospect Road our demographic screen identified three mission target groups for which Prospect Road Uniting Church could provide three outreach communities.

This kind of screen can work, even in seemingly monoculture communities. Many years ago, I was a member of a denominational team which went on deputation to some small towns in the Australian Outback. At a meeting in one small town, the matriarch of the congregation filled us in on what the town was like. "In this town," she said, "there are three kinds of people. There's Them, Those, and Us. 'Them' are the railway workers and aboriginals who live on the other side of the railway line; 'Those' are the schoolteachers, the state police, the bank manager, the stockbroker, and the storekeepers who live in the town and 'Us' are the ranchers. In this church, we don't have anything to do with 'Them,' 'Those' send their children to Sunday school, and 'Us' are the ones who run everything." I am sure it was an accurate demographic analysis of the town and the church. It is difficult to imagine this church ministering to "Them" and "Those" in anything but a highly patronizing way or of "Us" relinquishing control to allow the other groups any stake in the church. Potentially, however, there are three different outreach ministries in that small place. Clustering churches and working regionally could allow more focused ministry, if the "Us" in the next small town would give up their privileges, which come from inherited control.

The target groupings are often found at the second level of screening. A rural church on the edge of a tourist area, but part of a wider cluster, has developed a "niche" ministry as a Retreat Centre. The church in another town where the small rural hospital has a large aged care annex for dementia patients is developing a support ministry for the family careers of patients. Another small city church is set in the middle of a regional shopping center and is developing a ministry to small businesspeople, their employees, and their families. Demographic screening is a strong indicator of the kinds of outreach communities a church might create.

Psychosocial "zoning" and outreach

Secondly we considered how people process their life information and experience. There are many systems that are used for "sorting out" people in this way. Most of them are too complex and too individual to be useful for the kind of broad community development that is needed. At Prospect Road, we used three simple categories—head, heart, and gut—to help us develop our new outreach communities. "Head, heart, and gut" is a neat mnemonic, but there can be some confusion between "heart" and "gut" in Western minds because we locate feelings symbolically in the heart. Head, relational, and gut may be clearer.

- "Head" people value cognitive process. In expressing an opinion, they tend to say, "I think...." They appreciate information being presented logically. Ideas are their springboards for action.

- "Heart" or "Relational" people value relationships and their effect on their own image. They tend to say, "It looks like...." They appreciate information being presented in a way that honors the recipient. Status is a springboard for action.

- "Gut" people value feelings and experimentation. They tend to say, "I feel...." They appreciate information through its touch and feel. Intuition is their springboard for action.

The categories are not exclusive. Head people express feelings, gut people can be concerned about relationships, and heart people may be highly intelligent.

These three broad personality profiles are present in every community. To locate them as target groups, it is useful to use them as colors that further delineate the demographic groupings. From Huston Smith,[10] we know that university-educated professionals are predominantly "head," as a consequence of their success in the scientific rationalism of their professions. So neighborhoods which have demographics indicating higher numbers of people who have been university educated, are likely to be "head." In modern society, "head" predominates.

Every town and city has high-status and low-status areas. I worked for many years in a low-status suburb. Every time a miscreant who came from this area was apprehended, the suburb name was emblazoned in the news headline. When the criminal came from a high-status area, the suburb name would be buried in the text, if mentioned at all. This kind of discriminatory reporting happens often. It always raised the ire of the good people in a good neighborhood whose goodness was not recognized. Relationships, image, and status are more important for people in both low-status and high-status areas. In the emerging postmodern epoch, "heart" or "relational" may predominate.

Modern society has undervalued "gut" characteristics in people, so people for whom this is important tend to mask it in order to make progress in a predominantly "heady" world. So there are few "gut" areas. Sometimes there are the remnants of the hippie culture of the seventies still around. Greenwich Village in New York, or areas near Berkeley, California, have a global image of a "gut," artistic, creative, alternative lifestyle area. Sometimes the clues to such an area are subtler. In the Prospect Road "patch" there is an area of filled-in clay pits and brickworks that has been redeveloped with up-market housing, close to the city center. The people who "pioneer" these formerly low-status areas have a layer of "alternative lifestyle" beneath their up-market respectability.

At Prospect Road, this new level of screening confirmed two target groups: "head" people who are parents of small children in the middle of the patch and "heart" people at the low-status northern end, with a question mark over a "gut" target group among the scattering of alternative lifestyle and creative people in the middle and at the south end. But if "head" predominates, are all the head people who are not parents another target group?

Character-based "zoning" and outreach

A friend went to buy a house for his daughter, a student in another Australian city. He looked at one area and fell in love with it. He looked at the leafy streets; he enjoyed the corner coffee shop. The house was quirky and quaint, just right for a university student. What attracted him was the character of the area. It matched his values. It was easy to incorporate into his self-story. It was an area where he and his family would enjoy living. Character is something present in the streetscapes of an area. Character has its roots in the cultural heritage of an area. Character comes out in the shared stories about people and their relationship to place. Character is related to demography and psychosocial groupings but has its own distinctive qualities that are both individual and collective. Character is the look and feel of local culture.

At Prospect Road, we identified character-based zoning when we looked at the character of each of the centres in our multi-centre church and found there was a match between their character and that of the area in which they are located. In Christendom, church community and wider community were seamless. Both were caught up in the same historical events. The stories that are remembered in the church are likely to be similar to those that formed the culture of the area and reflect its values. The local church is a microcosm of the local neighborhood in which it was, and may still be, indigenous.

There are three ways in which we can use the information to be gleaned from considering a church's and hence a neighborhood's character. One is to treat character as a gift from the past to the present and future and re-jig it to make it relevant in its new social context. Leonard Sweet's concept of "ancient/future"[11] uses the character of the early Church to inform the character of the future Church, using liturgy as its medium. The same concept can be used to take the character trait of a church and contextualize it for the twenty-first century. Out of the five centres at Prospect Road, one has a character trait of risk-taking and working with young people, and one has a character trait of Sunday school and work with families and children. Two adjacent centres have a strong character trait of "people power." The fifth centre has a character trait of self-improvement.

Another gain from character-based zoning is to use the stories that contribute to character to empower change. Harrison Owen uses the concept of "mythos" to describe the kind of stories that can turn around an organization.[12] At one of the centres at

Prospect Road, I inherited an elderly Management Committee with a reputation for saying "No!" to everything. I discovered a story, "The Midnight Demolition Job," of how, in the past, a young go-ahead pastor had enlisted the youth group to come in the middle of the night to remove a tree and demolish a fence that the Trustees had refused to change. The members of the Management Committee had been members of that youth group. After re-appropriating the story to the present, they were surprisingly supportive of all the changes that we made!

Another way of using character is to gain an insight into how to witness to the area. Rolf Jensen writes about using an area's character and stories to tap into its aspirations. It is a way of focusing marketing for organizations.[13] We have been conscious of this in our publicity and brochures at Prospect Road. Also, when we upgraded one of the centres, we put twenty-first century flexibility and amenity into an early twentieth-century ambience; to match the way young families in the area are renovating the early twentieth-century housing in the area.

Not every aspect of character is helpful, as anyone knows who has been blocked by the challenge, "That's not the way we do things here!" Nevertheless, recognizing and contextualizing the elements of character in a church or area can give leverage for change by clothing the new with elements of what is loved, familiar, and energizing, by motivating change through remembering past courage and victories, and by finding new ways of getting our message seen and heard.

Mixed and matched for mission: a multi-campus church

We chose to match the two centres in the middle of the patch to the "head" people in that area. We assigned the ministry to the Gen-X families to the centre with a "victory story" of working with families and children and designated the other, with the character of self-improvement, as a center for learning. We matched the two centres at the low-status northern end of the patch to "heart" people in that area. The more centrally located of the two became the worship centre, the other a community centre. Finally, the centre at the south end with "victory stories of innovation and work with young people we matched with the alternative lifestyle, "gut" people in the area.

After further development and experience, the five Prospect Road centres became four communities—Parentlink, Learner-link, Neighborlink, and Innerlink. Each has a focused ministry and together offers "all things to all people, that we by all means save some." What has emerged through focusing on openness and mission is a new form of postmodern community and church.

---

[8]Roger Lewin, *Complexity: Life at the Edge of Chaos* (London: J.M. Dent, 1993), p. 44ff.

[9]Because "Congregation" is usually a prescribed entity in Church Constitutions and Rules, I have been careful to, in general, only use the word to describe this entity and "outreach community" to describe the gathered worshiping group of people at each of the multi-point centers of the church. This is important because it minimizes prescriptive behavior and thus gives the communities greater freedom to adopt innovative worship and mission outreach. The need to limit prescriptive behavior is examined in greater detail in Chapter 4.

[10]Huston Smith, p. 79ff.

[11]Leonard Sweet, *Aqua Church: Essential Leadership Arts for Piloting your Church in Today's Fluid Culture* (Loveland, C. Group Publishing, 1999), p. 81. See Chapter 5 on "Ancient/future Orienteering."

[12]Harrison Owen, *Spirit: Transformation and Development in Organizations* (Potomac: Abbott, 1987).

[13]Rolf Jensen, *The Dream Society: How the Coming Shift From Information To Imagination Will Transform Your Business* (New York: McGraw-Hill, 1999).

CHAPTER 2

Thriving in a Climate of Change

My call to ministry is to make the Church relevant to its mission field. Forty years ago I was working as a design draftsman in a small, isolated Australian mining town. A worker living in the men's barracks came home distraught in the middle of the night after a relationship break-up. He tried to wake a friend, but was unable, so he committed suicide. It was a small company town where everybody knew everybody. There was a resident Methodist clergyman and a Catholic priest. Why did the man not think to walk the short distance down the road to one pastor, or the short distance up the road to the other? I know that suicide is an irrational act, but the incident made me look at the effectiveness of the Church. If the Church had so little impact on a person's life in a place where we were all dependent on one another, when and where would it be relevant? So, trying to make the Church relevant to its local population has been at the heart of my ministry since first seeing the situation with life-changing clarity forty years ago.

I came into ministry at the very time the wheels were beginning to fall off the Church in Australia. The Church became a minor player in its local neighborhood affairs. We were being battered by a "storm front" of global change without any idea of how to respond. This "storm front" probably began to build up in Australia after World War I. In that period we found our nationhood, but many persons, by rejecting organized religion, resolved the paradox of Christendom by blessing both sides of a conflict, which was pure hell for all involved. In North America and

Europe, different influences had similar effect. The "front" became global. In the face of this storm change, the Church tried to do things better. That did not work. Then it tried strategic planning.

I am a head person. I love planning and do it well. But big new schemes for the Church did not work either. Fulfilling the plan was too time consuming, slow, and inflexible to fulfill the mission. It was an imposed top-down response, even when it was generated democratically, and rubbed in the wrong way every aspect of the new worldview that was coming into being.

LOCAL GUSTS AND EDDIES OF CHANGE

What we experienced first were the local gusts and eddies of change. These changes had always been around, but the pace of their coming was harder to absorb. We experienced things such as changing work patterns—women in the workforce, job insecurity, and the change from manufacturing to service jobs, demographic changes. We observed changing age cohorts and ethnicity in neighborhoods. We perceived changes in land use, including "gentrification" of low-income areas and social mobility. "Stable" neighborhoods turn over 20 percent of their population each year!

These changes often made a big difference in church life. To maintain stability over change, churches abandoned their sense of mission, allowed controllers to take over, faced financial and staffing crises, and often faced burnout in their key leaders. When we look back over a generation, we can see that these changes were significant. Often, these are the things that church people have blamed for the decline of their church. In shifting the problem away from themselves, they have avoided taking any alternative action. How often have we heard, or even said ourselves, "The problem is … ."? Change is not a problem but a fact. If there is a problem it is that the Church does not know how to change in response to the issues it faces in mission.

THE CLIMATE OF GLOBAL CHANGE

About fifteen years ago, I was ministering in a district where the local Catholic priest shared many of my interests and concerns. He introduced me to the book, *Evangelization and Justice—New Insights for Christian Ministry*, by John Walsh, a Maryknoll Missionary in Japan.[14] Walsh took the research on individual faith development by James Fowler[15] and applied it socially in a global framework. Walsh's viewpoint defines some clear characteristics for people living out of the worldviews of the past, present, and emerging epochs. Walsh also uses more accessible language than the postmodern philosophers. This makes it easier to explain global changes to local church people. But even though Walsh is clearer, he can still seem a bit too abstract. To remedy this, I have added my own catch- phrases in the table below to describe each stage.

The Stages of Faith Maturity[16]

Stage One	Intuitive–projective	Faith from parent	Get the "vibes" (moods and actions).
Stage Two	Mythic–literal	Faith from parents/parent substitute ("stories")	Be like your hero/heroine.
Stage Three	Synthetic–conventional	Faith from environment (group)	Do as you're told. Follow the band.
Stage Four	Individuating–reflexive	Individuals begin to be responsible for their own faith (polarities arise)	Do it yourself.
Stage Five	Conjunctive Paradoxical-consolidative	Individuals absorb from opposite polarities	Accompany others.
Stage Six	Universalizing	Resolution/superanimation of all polarities	Find Christ in everything.

Stage Three, "Do as you're told" or "Follow the band" is a way of conceptualizing the modern epoch. Stage Four, "Do it yourself," is the postmodern epoch, although I think "postmodern" is still developing. When it matures, this current epoch will have a more definitive name and perhaps, because of the influence of relativism, have more Stage Five, "Accompany others" characteristics.

Walsh suggests, following Fowler, that the changes that identify the different epochs are developmental and incremental. Since each stage grows out of and includes the previous stages, a fully developed Stage Five faith should be able to operate out of the gifts and insights of the previous stages. However, in history as in individual maturing, the impetus to appropriate the new often comes at the expense of the rejection and denial of the old. This is reflected in the experience of the congregation. The church has been identified as belonging to the "Do as you're told" epoch by postmoderns and to the "Be like your hero/heroine" epoch by both modern and postmodern people. Walsh's theory offers a more inclusive future for our mission but does not reflect the reality of the hostility and distrust that is being encountered.

LOCAL MINISTRY AND GLOBAL CHANGE

Ministry in a hostile mission field

Huston Smith in *Why Religion Matters: The Fate Of the Human Spirit In an Age of Disbelief* [17] looks at the climate of change differently. His book is an apology for the religious or traditional worldview—his name for the period before modernity—and is a critique of modernity and the refusal of scientific rationalism to give any credence or value to a religious worldview. Huston Smith leaves us in no doubt that the world in which we minister is hostile toward religion and hence toward the Church. He exposes the extent of this hostility and tries by persuasively arguing a case for a religious worldview alongside a scientific/ rationalist one, to have people who are immersed in that worldview reconsider the worth and purpose of religion. As we consider our mission to the modern world, Huston Smith opens us to its reality. To minister to the modern world we will need to overcome our relegation to insignificance and learn how to penetrate the wall of latent and sometimes overt hostility that we face. We know, from this book, what we are up against and it is daunting. His insights into modernism make our situation clear.

We have a difficult missionary task ahead of us.

Once, the Church held a position of respect and influence in local society, but no longer. Now people keep quiet about their faith in the face of hostile attitudes and other indicators of the low social status of the Church. Irrespective of the internal strength and faith of the Church, or individual Christians, we have to build relationships and evangelize from a position of weakness. Huston Smith discusses the role of the media in championing scientific rationalism over religion,[18] and he demonstrates how difficult it has become to argue for one's Christian beliefs. Such a discussion is likely to descend from science versus religion, to evolution versus creation, to intelligence, open-mindedness, and progress versus ignorance, bigotry, and backward-looking, to you versus me. This is a no-contest, no-win situation for Christian witness. Books on church growth sometimes urge Christians to invite friends, neighbors, fellow workers, and family members to church. In Australia, even dedicated Christians will not risk the potential damage such asking could do to important relationships. The situation may be different in North America. Huston Smith quotes a quip by Peter Berger that implies that while the leadership elites in North America are anti-religious, the masses are not.[19] This is not true for Australia. In our history, secularity has always been prominent. The anti-religion sentiments of scientific rationalism have found fertile ground here.

In a way, the Church is reaping the harvest of its own vitriolic criticism of both the pre-reformation Church and the religions it found in conquered nations in its missionary alliance with colonialism. The Church gave scientific rationalism the attitude and the language that is now being used against it. When the modern epoch came into being, the Church was part of the change process and pattern. The Church of Protestantism in all its variety (and Catholicism in response) became profoundly different from the Church of the Middle Ages. The Church evolved and took on the form it needed to thrive in the new epoch. Now, on the other side of the peak of the ascendancy of the modernist worldview, the Church needs to evolve and reinvent itself for the emerging epoch. Postmodernism is the vehicle of this change.

Ministry in a distrustful mission field

Huston Smith has little to say about postmodernism. He sees it, like modernism, to be in opposition to tradition and religion. However, Huston Smith's brief remarks are helpful in that they identify three key issues of postmodernism that work against the Church as it is now, thus giving us some beginning points for change. The following table lists them along with some simplified terminology that will help us identify our distrustful mission field.[20]

Postmodern Culture's Climate of Distrust

Incredulity toward meta-narratives	Distrust of authority
No consensual worldview	Distrust of ideology
Deconstruction	Distrust of systems
Hermeneutics of suspicion	Distrust of motives

Distrust of Authority

A young, female parent remarked, "You won't catch me going to listen to some old man telling me what to do out of a book!" She spoke for every Gen Xer. Unless we take seriously the aversion that postmoderns feel toward "Church-as-authority," our efforts to recruit them into church community will fail. The strategy of Christendom churches to rely on "guilt-tripping" and other pressures to conform does attract people who feel vulnerable, or confused, or duty-bound. In times of rapid change, there are more vulnerable and confused people. Authoritarianism "certainty" works for them for a while. To use Walsh's categories, there are still plenty of Stage Three, "Do as you're told" people around. But the prevailing postmodern belief radically questions authority, so an authoritarian approach will be less and less productive as Christendom dissolves.

Distrust of Ideology

The distrust of ideology means that four hundred years of doctrinal distinctiveness that defines the denominational character of local ministry has very little credence in a postmodern mission field. Competition between denominations on the secular, hostile mission field is now as pointless as ecumenical cooperation. Denomi-national doctrine helps form the distinctive character of any particular church, along with the influences of its cultural setting and the ministry skills it values. If this "mix" resonates with an individual, or another church, then some kind of mutual engagement in mission will happen, even though, theologically, they may be poles apart. Missiology is more important than theology in our time.

Personal witness will change too. Much of the "faith talk" of Christians on the mission field is loaded with doctrinal "tags"— words and phrases that in Christendom identified the theological "tribe" to which the person belonged. If a hearer responded to the language, they were part of the tribe and their faith could be encouraged and grown. If not: disengagement. Postmoderns are conscious of these tags and do not respond to them because they distrust that kind of "blanket" doctrinal inclusive/exclusiveness. What they respond to is the being and action of the person. Later, they may make sense of the doctrine, but first they need to resonate with the person or the church. Even then, if that relationship "drops out" for any reason, the next engagement, if it occurs, is just as likely to be in (in Christendom terms) a church with an opposite doctrinal stance as one that is the same as their previous church.

Distrust of Systems

Postmodern distrust of systems works as much for the Church as against it. "Deconstruction" will critique modernism as well as religion and, in time, open up a new way of being that incorporates elements of both. Deconstruction allows situations to remain paradoxical without being collapsed into either opposing view. Deconstruction offers a different model than the conflict of dialectic to deal with opposing, seemingly irreconcilable positions. In a time of rapid and continuing change, deconstruction offers a way of moving with the flow of change and evolving a new "system" that, because it is always in question and changing, is scarcely a system as we know it. Huston Smith is right in seeing that it threatens the traditional religious worldview, but modernism has done that already. It offers a way beyond modernism that can include subjective realities and hence allow the development of new forms of fellowship with Jesus. Jesus remains central because he is always there as a basic reality of Church, however much "system" is stripped away.

Distrust of Motives

The fourth postmodern issue is the distrust of motives. This affects relationships by making personal acceptance harder to earn and to give. Both the other person's and one's own motives need to be checked and reconciled as a necessary process in relationship building. This means that postmoderns connect in a different way. They leave a small space between themselves and others that needs a "leap of faith" to bridge before a relationship is established. As life changes, the space comes back and needs a new leap of faith to re-establish connection. Loyalty is low for postmoderns. It needs to be earned and re-earned.

In modern or Christendom community, connections were seen as once-in-a-lifetime events. During most times, community was maintained by common rules, controls, sanctions, loyalties, and expectations. Because in postmodern community these influences are largely rejected, every experience that challenges postmoderns to be in community recreates a gap requiring a new falling in love or a new leap of faith.

How can you build community when community members think that showing up once every five or six weeks is "commitment?" Intermittent attendance is another form of "gap." In our Australian secular, postmodern, and post-Christendom culture, people who participate intermittently are committed. Community will not come by regularity but by immediacy. Every attendance needs to count. High energy, spiritual discernment, and a congruency of church and personal mission are the qualities that will call forth a leap of faith.

THE SMALL CHURCH AT LARGE IN A CHANGING MISSION FIELD

When I went to the small mining community I described at the beginning of this chapter, I went from one of Australia's driest state capitals to one of its wettest small communities. The change was enormous. But because I wanted the work that was available to me there, I adjusted. I adjusted to a small company town and thrived. I adjusted to being far away from familiar people and thrived. I went from a climate with 20 inches of annual rainfall to a climate with 132 inches of annual rainfall, and I thrived—permanently attached to the largest and most robust umbrella I could find! I thrived, at large in an alien environment, because I wanted to do the work that was there more than I wanted to keep the familiarity of hometown and the comfort of a sunny climate. And God was there to call me and lead me. In our times, we need to love the mission so much that we are willing to leave the comforts of Christendom and move into a hostile, distrustful, irreligious mission field. And God will be there to call us and lead us.

Undaunted by hostility

Paulo Freire, in *Pedagogy of the Oppressed* [21] sets out a revolutionary's view of how to deal with a hostile and oppressive system. Sifting through the revolutionary rhetoric in a fairly "dry" translation is hard work, but his understanding of alienation and indigenous learning can be applied differently and helpfully in the mission outreach of the Church in our times. There is a risk that the revolutionary schema endorsed by Freire will so color what we read that we miss the value we can take from his thought and lose sight of effective strategies for thriving in a hostile mission field. Frieire's schema has three phases—concientization, pedagogy, and dialogue.

Concientization is the process of "waking up" the "oppressed" to the nature of the system that is oppressing them. Revealing the true nature of the seemingly overwhelming influences that are maintaining the oppression to which they are subject can stimulate people and arouse them from apathy and helplessness. Huston Smith's book, for example, admirably fulfills this task for religion. The pedagogy phase helps the oppressed see that they have within themselves qualities and gifts that have not been developed and recognized by "the system." With Freire, the major tool in the task of pedagogy is literacy. Literate people obtain the means of express-

ing their feelings and understandings about their situation and entering into a dialogue with the oppressing forces. Perhaps, in our situation of a hostile and distrustful mission field, spirituality is the
experiential and sensory "language" that is needed to dialogue with
scientific rationalism. Finally, dialogue is not the confrontational
dialectic with its overtones of violence that recent history has
demonstrated can easily become a hurtful and ineffective "blunt
instrument" for change, but rather residing in Stage Five, "Accompanying Others," by living with the paradoxical, deconstructive kind
of dialogue that postmodernism offers.

Sometimes the awakening and ownership of a religious worldview happens in the midst of hostility and opposition. People
respond to "the vibes" or live out of an almost forgotten story in a
Stage One or Stage Two faith experience.

> Lyn is a Catholic chaplain in a university. She is also a
> funeral celebrant. She approaches both roles with an attitude
> of service, not one of dumping a pile of dogma on to the other
> person expecting them to conform in some way, but asking
> the question of one who serves the other—"What do you
> want? How can I help?"
>
> Recently she was conducting a funeral and came to plan the
> ceremony with a small group of friends and relatives who
> wanted a funeral "without the God bits." In planning the
> funeral she assured them that there was nothing they "had to
> do," and asked, "So what would you like to do?" They ended
> up deciding to sit in a circle, each with something symbolic of
> the deceased, each remembering him in his or her own way.
> The people were so involved in this celebration of the person's
> life that the time flew past and they eventually had to be
> asked to leave the chapel for the next service! It was a won-
> derful, uplifting time. Lyn says, "It's amazing how often in
> planning the funeral they start off by saying that they 'don't
> want any God bits' and end up with the Lord's Prayer or some
> piece of Scripture, or something. They don't know I'm
> Catholic . . . I just ask what they want and help them think
> through the service."

Jesus' reply to the Pharisees at his entry into Jerusalem
reminds us of how faith happens in spite of a hostile mission
field. "Some of the Pharisees in the crowd said to him, 'Teacher,

order your disciples to stop.' He answered, 'I tell you, if these were silent, the stones would shout out.'"[22]

There is something in existence itself that rejoices in faith, as some scientists are now admitting, but it is not rejoicing in "Church" or any other religious institution, but rather in a personal and general "spirituality." This is a cause for hope. With a lot more sensitivity and finesse than we have sometimes shown in the past, it should be possible to evangelize through spirituality, leaving engagement with Church as a much more open question. This is discussed in greater detail in Chapter Three.

There is power in "the vibes" or the oft-repeated stories in a Stage One or Stage Two faith experience. In circumstances where opposition to religion is organized and violent, faith at this level not only allows the Church to survive but to thrive as well. Bill Easum quotes these figures in *Leadership on the Other Side.*

> When Mao-tse-Tung took over, there were two million Christians in China. His regime killed the missionaries, arrested the pastors, shut down the churches, and persecuted the Christians. When he died there were fifty million known Christians in China.[23]

Christians still face persecution in China. The opposition is overt, so Christians are "awake" to the realities of their mission field and respond with a courage and integrity that brings a "lived" gospel to those looking for faith.

In safer, more open societies, raising the church's profile in the neighborhood can signal a new awareness and responsiveness of the church to people's interests or concerns, and then challenge their stereotypes. The testimony of a young mother in the Parent/Child strand of worship at Prospect Road, "Being in worship (here) is quality family time," is the kind of story to share. Networking can also raise the church's profile with all the other groups and organizations working with the church's mission target group. At Prospect Road, the Parentlink Community networked with childcare centres, community centres, kindergartens, playgroups, and schools.

It is easy to fall into the trap of responding to hostility with hostility and to "demonize" the mission field. It is helpful to remind ourselves that we have been called by God to be who we are, which is to be like Jesus, where we are. Our mission field, whatever its hostility towards the Church, is the gift that God has given and an opportunity to serve faithfully.

> Spirituality is to an oppressed religious sense what literacy is to the oppressed poor in Freire's schema. It is a "do it yourself," Stage Four expression of faith. Spirituality uses spiritual constructs and exercises to find and explore a deep, personal relationship with Jesus and God, in a similar way that Freire's pedagogy uses word constructs and meanings to find and explore socio-political relationships. Spirituality is not just specific events but a way of being Church in which discernment of God's leading has as much bearing on what happens as plans and logic. Being a multi-campus small church like Prospect Road can provide dedicated space to conduct forms of spirituality that could be threatening to traditional worshipers sharing the same space.

In Australia, a number of small churches have set up spirituality centres with classic meditation, contemplation, and prayer, including exercises based on non-Christian disciplines like Zen and Yoga. Others have set up retreat centres as "occasional" spirituality centres. Relaxation classes can be "entry level" encounters with spirituality. At Prospect Road we have set up or are in the process of setting up programs involving regular opportunities for dialogue with Jesus and God through Scripture reflection, intercessory prayer, and focused listening for revelation, including a Friday evening, mealtime, small-group service that constructs contemplative installations, creates prayers, poems, and songs and devises movements. It borrows from classic spirituality and popular culture. It uses a flexible space with multimedia projection and hi-fi sound.

Spiritually literate

Pedagogy is the phase between concientization and dialogue in Freire's scheme for dealing with oppression. In adapting this schema to deal with the oppression of the religious worldview by scientific rationalism, we too need to consider how we coach our church people to change from being oppressed to being at large. Freire's pedagogy stresses two educational qualities that are needed to prepare the oppressed for dialogue. The first concerns the teacher–pupil relationship. Modernist education presumes that the pupil is an empty jug to be filled from the wellsprings or "bank" of knowledge that the teacher possesses. But this discounts the knowledge that the pupil brings to the pedagogy—knowledge gained from his or her own experience of life. So pedagogy should be a combination of teacher as teacher, pupil as pupil, teacher as pupil, and pupil as teacher. The second concerns action and reflection. The beginning point for the reflection is the practical accomplishments of life and work (and in our case, religion). So literacy for bricklayers begins with the word brick and extends to the materials and building methods that are a familiar strength of their knowledge. The object of the pedagogy is to give the oppressed the language, concepts, and confidence they need to engage in dialogue with their oppressors.

For the small church to be equipped to thrive in its changing mission field requires a similar pedagogical shift. To do this at Prospect Road we were greatly assisted by the books and online teaching of Easum, Bandy, and Associates. Their coaching ministry follows similar concepts to those of Freire. They start with current church praxis—going from the strong and familiar to the new and entrepreneurial—and provide tools and concepts to build common understanding of a way forward. Their critics sometimes assert that the advice emerges from and pertains to the postmodern, very large church. However, Prospect Road, a small church, was able to change as I worked through three books. Each book uses metaphors that help to ground radical concepts in familiar imagery.

The first book, *Sacred Cows Make Gourmet Burgers,*[24] uses the metaphor of cows wandering the streets of India's towns and villages. The cows are sacred and cannot be used for food while at the same time people suffer because of lack of protein. Easum uses this metaphor to catalogue, with a wry sense of humor, the people, and ways of congregational life that have become sacred and untouchable. These attitudes and practices consume resources and deny people access to what should be there to spiritually feed them. I first read this book at a time when I was trying to deal with a herd of sacred cows. The book helped me personally to own the reality of my frustration, to see the extent to which the church was being hindered, and to be encouraged to devise ways to change the situation: We made a few gourmet burgers! This book is in itself part of the concientization of the church to its predicament but then goes on to coach the church in developing ways to move forward. We did not use this book as a direct coaching tool at Prospect Road, but it helped me lead the process of facing our ineffectiveness as a church and plucking up the courage to begin to change. Later, when we began to implement the new administrative system at Prospect Road, we used the coaching on permission-giving churches, leaders, and teams that are a key insight of this book.

The book we used to coach us through the start-up period of planting the first new communities at Prospect Road was *Growing Spiritual Redwoods*,[25] which Bill Easum wrote with Tom Bandy. Radical reorganization was our bold first move. We amalgamated the original five small congregations into one and established four new outreach communities in their place. We had to deal with grieving and a sense of loss, but did not let denial or anger block the forward thrust of our change. Establishing a traditional worship service first helped provide enough familiarity to alleviate people's worst fears of change and yet enough innovation to encourage those who were ready to move to plant our new communities in the vacated centres. *Growing Spiritual Redwoods* coached us through this change.

The book uses familiar and accessible metaphors. The metaphor of "tall timber" encouraged us to look to see a horizon above and beyond "the "undergrowth" of all that was new and confusing. The metaphor of the "forest path" encouraged us to move on through our uncertainties. The metaphor of "the midwife" helped us see our own role and purpose in helping to bring the future church into being. The organic metaphors of "tree, heartwood, and sap" brought home to us the change from a mechanistic worldview to an organic.

God was good to us at Prospect Road. Bill Easum visited

Australia at the very time we needed his coaching most. We were able to take a group of leaders to his presentation to reinforce the book's coaching. *Growing Spiritual Redwoods* is a good "beginners" book in the process of church transformation, but there is much to interest and excite those who are further advanced. Easum and Bandy provide profound insights into the future for small churches in ways that are helpful. Some of the multiple choice worship options at Prospect Road, such as multi-sensory worship, were inspired from this book, as were our organizational changes from committees to teams.

We all grow and change at different rates, and the task of coaching needs to extend to include all those who are part of the church's life. Easum stimulated the leaders. Others were stimulated by the changes themselves as they happened. Bit by bit we coached the established churchgoers to change from seeing the church as "being there for them" to seeing the church as "being there for mission." They were helped to understand the spiritual needs of those outside the church, and as a consequence, to refine the community's worship and activities to respond to those needs. They began to unlearn habits and offputting behaviors and practices. Just as prayer was an important aspect of the beginning of our changes at Prospect Road, so we found that coaching people to be more confident in their relationship with Jesus and God was an important learning task.

Bill Easum's subsequent book, *Leadership on the Other Side*,[26] uses the metaphor of time/space travel to help us gain a sense that, by finding the right opening in the universe (a wormhole in space), we can zip through it into the future. This book takes the insights of *Growing Spiritual Redwoods* to another level but at the expense of accessibility. More people understand trees, forests, and midwives than space travel, but the new levels of sophistication in this book are important for pastors and key leaders to grasp. The table below, from page 39, not only lists the contents of each chapter in the book but the beginning and endpoint of the "coaching session" each chapter contains.

The Challenge of Our Times

"What was" Life Metaphors	"What is emerging" Life Metaphors
Matter	Spirit
Mechanical	Organic
Institutional	Spiritual
Church	*Kin*-dom
Committees	Teams
Entitled and Elected	Called Servants
European Command and Control	Indigenous Permission Giving
Command and Control	Permission Giving

These "lessons" were important in reinforcing what we had initiated at Prospect Road. Fractalling is a key insight of this book and goes to the heart of how pedagogy might work in an organic way. Fractalling and permission-giving organization for the small church will be considered in greater depth in Chapter Four.

Using distrust as a tool

The third phase of Freire's schema for breaking free from oppression is dialogue. In our adaptation of Freire to deal with the oppression of the religious worldview by modernist, scientific rationalism, we too will need to consider how we deal with this phase. Dialectic is the form that Freire and Huston Smith use. But, in spite of the instances from Huston Smith, of scientific individuals and modernist institutions expanding their vision to include subjective experience as an important consideration in their worldview, the general outcome is denial and hostility. The same can be said of Freire's more revolutionary dialectic. The confrontation between the oppressed and their oppressors can lead to violence, as Freire acknowledges. We have seen too much pain and suffering from this form of "dialogue" to give it any credence as a Christian strategy. In addition, too often, even when the oppressed "succeed" through violence, the confrontation continues, often with those formerly oppressed becoming the new oppressors. Dialogue becomes a tussle between two, competing

"Do as you're told" ideologies, and this polarization is discredited in postmodern times.

Rather than adopt dialectic as the way to dialogue with scientific rationalism and in order to break out from its oppression, we should look at how the emerging worldview of postmodernism dialogues with modernism. Four hundred years ago, the Reformation was the label given to the period and process during which the Church used the emerging rationalist worldview to evolve. The Church as we know it today, both Protestant and Catholic, is the product of that evolutionary process. Now, we need to evolve once more through using postmodern praxis as the basis of a dialogue with modernism that will free the Church from its oppression.

Postmodern distrust is the sign of a worldview that has been "conscientized" to the oppressive aspects of the modern worldview and the complicity of its victims in their own oppression. The postmodern challenge to four objects of that distrust—authority, ideology, systems, and motives—is the basis of the understanding we need to evolve and emerge as a new Church in a new epoch.

Distrust of authority is the first awakening point. The Church, in its Christendom, modernist form needs to dialogue through postmodern incredulity toward all worldviews in the ways they present themselves. For the small local church this means recasting many of the ways we witness in society. When the words "Church" and denomination appear in advertising and signage, we signal a modernist authority. At Prospect Road, our dialogue around this issue suggests that we should downplay tags and feature relational groupings instead. Tradition implies another form of authority, so we have avoided using the word traditional to describe our "old style" worship. We use the word classic instead. The same thing applies to describing the historical gifts of our Church. We use the word *heritage* instead of *tradition*. *Classic* and *heritage* are better words and images for postmoderns.

During moments of church dialogue about forthcoming changes, the choice of question is crucial. Frame the questions like this: Will we "Do it Ourselves?" Or will we "Do as we're told?" Or will we "Follow the band?" By changing this question in the small church, we were able to to promote interactive worship and learning. We made decision-making transparent and participatory. We gave people choices and freedom to choose. We avoided the feeling of "capture" by discerning the time to ask for personal information, which made it as easy to leave as it was to enter. Every one of these strategies contradicts the tenets of Christendom churches.

Paradoxically, the distrust of ideologies and systems calls for a greater trust in one another. The fact that two ideologies, or two churches are similar is less important than pragmatic mutuality. Beneficial relationships are forged on the mission field as each is enabled to be a better "missionary." At Prospect Road, we work successfully with two groups, each with different ideologies from one another. But for each party, the relationship enriches outreach and allows far more to be accomplished than could happen if ideological agreement had to be recognized or negotiated first. The dialogue with modernism through the postmodern tool of deconstruction has allowed people to look through and beyond ideological differences and find enough basic elements like Jesus, God's love, and congruency with Scripture to be able to reconstruct a relationship that in Christendom would never be considered. By using an organic metaphor, postmodernism opens up a kind of spiritual bio-diversity in which new and effective ministry relationships occur and from which a new expression of "Church" will emerge—networked, transmorphic, and multi-faceted Church.

Distrust of motives provokes dialogue on the nature of commitment and belonging. Examples of distrust include discipleship concepts or covenants such as "once in a lifetime," "commitment," and membership oaths that are central to Christendom and that invoke feelings of "Do as you're told" and "Follow the band," or even, "Will you be loyal . . . " These oaths are challenged by a kind of commitment that is tied to relationships, to circumstances and situations that the postmodern distrust has checked and approved. As the relationships, circumstances, and situations change, commitment is reassessed. Membership implies being "locked in" and obligated for postmoderns, and thus it is less and less likely to be embraced. Commitment shows up in actual, meaningful engagement with the congregation.

This conversation could be repeated with respect to marriage, or the commitment made by parents at infant baptism and dedications. Usually, at marriage ceremonies I conduct, the vows are repeated line for line, but occasionally a couple wishes to memorize their vows. I met with one bride, years later, who had done this. She testified to how helpful it had been for her to be able to recall her vows and use them to "commit" to her marriage as her relationships, circumstances, and situation changed. Perhaps covenants need to be more like mantras that can be recalled to signify recommitment to relationships that are reassessed because of change. In the new sense of commitment, openness will be more effective than obligations, rules, and sanctions in sustaining connection. The Old Testament book of Exodus is helpful. How many times in that story did Moses have to call the people to commit to God? He called as many times as the situation changed.

There are further implications for small churches. Whenever changes in personnel—pastor, staff, or key leaders—occur, the induction processes should provide opportunity to assess the new relationships, circumstances, and situation. Openness is key, and this is paradoxical to the confidentiality required in negotiations to fill pastor or staff vacancies. In Christendom churches, it is presumed that "the system" or the "connection" will hold things together, rather than the local setting. This presumption can no longer be maintained.

In the absence of a single benchmark experience and ritual that signifies being in or out of the Church, is there anything we can look for in a person that indicates commitment besides "being there?" I believe there are four universally discernable "turning points" of commitment that are checked out by distrustful postmoderns. They are:

1. Engagement in mutually rewarding relationship (with Jesus, partner, fellow-worker, children, friends)
2. The recognition and affirmation of being held in the highest regard (by God, partner, parents, children, friends)
3. The change from "What's in it for me?" to "What can I do to help?"

4. Responding with one's life to the discernment of one's life purpose (the call of God)

These perceptions look very similar to Christendom's marks of membership. We should expect this. Just as Newton's Laws in physics were subsumed by relativity, so with these turning points. Membership in Christendom was determined and fixed by rules. These are relative to the relationships, circumstances, and situation at the time. These four "signs" of commitment are the basis for the outreach strategy I discuss in Chapter 3.

---

[14] John Walsh M.M, *Evangelization and Justice: New Insights For Christian Ministry* (Maryknoll, NY: Orbis, 1982).

[15] James W. Fowler, *Stages of Faith: The Psychology of Human Development and the Quest for Meaning* (Harper and Row, 1982). My copy published by Dove Walsh is much more cogent with his thesis than Fowler is himself in his own book on the subject, in *Weaving the New Creation: Stages of Faith and the Public Church* (Harper SanFrancisco, 1991).

[16] John Walsh, p. 4.

[17] Huston Smith, *Why Religion Matters.*

[18] Smith, Chapter 6, "The Tunnel's Roof: The Media," p. 193ff.

[19] Smith, p. 103.

[20] Smith, pp. 20, 89 respectively. I have oversimplified the full meaning of these major aspects of postmodernism for the sake of identifying the kinds of ministry approach we will need to deal with postmodernism. For a good overview of postmodernism, refer to Stuart Sim, editor, *The Icon Critical Dictionary of Postmodern Thought* (Cambridge UK: Icon Books, 1998).

[21] Paulo Freire, *Pedagogy of the Oppressed* (Sheed and Ward, 1972).

[22] Luke 19:39, 40.

[23] William Easum, *Leadership on the Other Side* (Nashville: Abingdon, 2000) p. 157.

[24] Easum, *Sacred Cows Make Gourmet Burgers* (Nashville: Abingdon, 1995).

[25] Easum and Thomas Bandy, *Growing Spiritual Redwoods* (Nashville: Abingdon, 1997).

[26] Easum, *Leadership On The Other Side*; Portal 4, "The Mother Life Metaphor" p. 82ff; Table, "The Challenge of our Times" p. 39.

CHAPTER 3

Open Gates
to Greener Pastures of Spirit

In the early 1970s, I was a minister in the Congregational Church (before it became part of the Uniting Church) in a small rural community. My church was the only church known locally by its denominational name. The other three local churches were labeled according to the European roots of the immigrants who had been their foundation members. So there was the English Church, the German Church, and the Irish Church. A few people chose their church on the basis of doctrinal correctness, a few others on worship or leadership style, but for most, unless there had been some major family or community trauma, there was little choice of church. People were born into their church communities. Family, clan, and denominational loyalties were strong in the Australian rural communities. Though the denominational identity (e.g. Lutheran, Reformed, Brethren, etc.) may have been more emphasized, similar patterns of ethnicity among small congregations are well documented in twentieth-century North America.

Very few of these values influence choice of church today. In Australia, a secular, anti-church culture dominates clan and family loyalties. Less than 10 percent of the Australian population has an active connection with a Christian church, and at every recent census, denominational identification has declined and "no religion" increased. Similar numbers are reported in Canada and Europe for an active connection with a church. The participation claims are higher in the United States, perhaps in the range of 25 percent, but the US will probably catch up with other societies as it becomes more secular and more hostile to religion. Something more than "denomination" or "doctrine" or even "worship and leadership style" will be needed to increase the likelihood of engagement with a congregation in the twenty-first century.

In the Prologue and the first two chapters, we looked at how the small church might change to meet the different kind of world in which it finds itself. In this chapter we turn to consider from their perspective, how persons might engage with such a church. At this level of complexity it is difficult to describe what people seeking to engage with Spirit might discover. The examples from Prospect Road are indicative only and are incomplete because the work there is incomplete. That understanding, in itself, is a sign of our times. There will be no settled, known, and replicable form of postmodern church. Change and responding to it, and Jesus, are the only constants in our time.

THE CHURCH IS "SPIRIT ON OFFER"

A person will engage with a church to engage with Spirit. Everything else he or she may need in life he or she can get outside a church, but only the Church has Spirit. People from other world religions may protest at this point. Mosques and temples may have Spirit too, but not the Spirit of Jesus. That is what we have different from others, and we need to appreciate what we have. We may have fellowship, or programs to help people, but Spirit is the key ingredient. People who know nothing about religion would not put the name of Jesus to it. They do not know Jesus—yet! They just know that in the midst of all that life holds, if they were to find Spirit anywhere, they should find it in a church. Even in places where people are dependent on charity groups run by the church, beyond their material needs is the need to engage with Spirit. Sometimes Spirit is the key need. A colleague of mine with extensive experience with church-based welfare agencies always developed strong and open links between the agency's clients and the local church so that Spirit might be found as well as food or shelter. So we should be clear in our offer to our mission target groups. Here is a place and here are people where you can find Spirit.

Peter Kahrimanis is a Greek, Pentecostal evangelist who works with us in a "side by side" ministry at Prospect Road. Sometimes his way of working puzzles us. In his evangelistic ministry to the least able people of our neighborhood, he offers surplus food from a food seller, free to all who come to take it. We were concerned that this would enmesh people in dependency, not lift them out of it. Apart from learning some good things about "control" and how easy it is to slip into that kind of relationship, Peter shared his mission strategy. His simple message is, "God is generous. God provides. This food is from God. Take it! No strings attached." We still feel uncomfortable about his perspective, but the message is simple, clear, and concrete. "God is generous! See for yourself." Of course there is more, such as teaching, love, and strategies to change and deal with compulsive behavior. The "food" relationship opens a gate to a Spirit relationship. Peter's strategy is not one we would have adopted, but its process is worth using. Be straightforward and concrete about Spirit in outreach so that Spirit can be key in the process of changing people's lives.

Finding ways to be "All things to all people that some might be saved," like St. Paul,[27] has been a major feature of our mission outreach strategy. By making available a number of different kinds of church experience to people, we increase our chances of making Spirit accessible. As well as offering choice, a multi-centre, multi-community, small church can focus its attention on specific target groupings. Previously I suggested three ways to screen the mission field: 1) demography, 2) psychosocial grouping, and 3) considering the character of the neighborhood and its relationship with the character of each church building and church community. These three parameters can be used to focus how we present Spirit. This external focus allows an internal focus too. Each centre covers only a part of the overall outreach of the church. Leaders and people with an interest in and excitement about what their centre is doing become, in themselves, tangible evidence of Spirit at work. By focusing each centre, we can expect higher energy to result, to the benefit of the church, but also for the potential benefit of those seeking Spirit there.

We have also begun to turn the church around to face the changes and difficulties of our times, and although this has meant that we need to do things differently, church is still a place of Spirit for the neighborhood. The church has changed and must change to do mission outreach effectively, but amidst many differences, Jesus remains the same. We must change the packaging, the images, and the concepts of the church that were part of its old being, because these have become off-putting to people in our time, but Jesus and Scripture remain primary elements of who we are and what we do. Behind the advertising, the networking, and our other efforts to engage people, Spirit remains the reason and the purpose of what we do.

As neighborhoods become increasingly secular and anti-church, so much of our interest and effort is focused on overcoming cultural barriers to faith that we could forget those who have stayed with Church in spite of the cultural pressures. We need to recognize these pressures and give some time to helping our church people relocate Spirit amidst all the changes. For some, the new style of church that we are developing at Prospect Road and inviting small churches to work on in their own cultural settings mean that Spirit, almost overly familiar in its old setting, may need to be "discovered" again.

SEARCHING FOR GREENER PASTURES

The vehicles proposed for offering Spirit to people are three or four outreach communities, each of them focused to minister to selected target groups. Let us now give our attention to the question, "Why would people in these groups want to engage with Spirit?" It is important to work out answers, so that our public offering of Spirit is effective in our centres and from our outreach communities. With multiple Centres we can both focus on a specific offering of Spirit for a target group and breadth through having a range of options. Those seeking Spirit will gather personal packages for themselves with one aspect of Spirit gleaned from one centre added to that gleaned from another. At Prospect Road, people are growing increasingly comfortable about moving about the centres and engaging in the different worship services, events, and activities they need to grow their faith.

In Chapter One we used three "screens" to identify our outreach target groups at Prospect Road and grew four communities to bring Spirit to them. Let us revisit these "screens" and the identifiers we used and see what might color a personal search for Spirit. The screens are used so that we can draw out the motivations toward Spirit and nuance the way that Spirit may appear as a "greener pasture" than where they are. This reintroduces the open sheep farm metaphor from the Prologue. In that story, the farmer, Robert, opened all his gates in times of drought, and because there was food and water everywhere on his property, the sheep could move to greener pastures when the paddock or field where they were grazing became bare and dry. What we are looking for in these different screens are the ways that spiritual "dryness" might be experienced. This will give us clues about presenting people with opportunities to find and move to "greener pastures" of Spirit.

Psychosocial zoning and Spirit

The simple mnemonic of head, heart, and gut that was used earlier will be less helpful here. In the motivation to seek Spirit, it is better to use the affective components of head, heart, and gut, which are: rational, relational, and experiential. However, we should remember that these categories are not mutually exclusive. Every search will involve rationality, relationships, and experiences. Psychosocial zoning identifies dominant influences. Spirit can then be offered in a way that remedies any spiritual dryness arising in that psychosocial grouping.

"Rational" people value ideas. This value predominates in most of our neighborhoods and is intrinsic to most Protestant churches because rationality is a controlling influence in modernity and also in the post-reformation Church. In rapidly changing times, many of the old rational constructs and doctrines that held life together no longer work, leaving a sense of ignorance and irrelevance that can be a kind of spiritual "dryness." Postmodern, "Do it yourself" people experience spiritual dryness in modern, "Do as you're told" rationality. Postmoderns responded with deconstruction, suspicion, and living with paradox. Their "dryness" comes from individualistic isolation and the lack of a more "relational" spirituality. Also, scientific rationality may not provide a satisfactory answer to, "Who am I?" The spiritual search arising from this kind of "dryness" may lead to an exploration of mystery, mysticism, and experiential spirituality.

"Relational" people are different, as I once discovered in a practical, personal, and slightly embarrassing way. I wanted to balance my "rational" nature with some "relational" spirituality, so I became a Lay Associate of the Missionaries of the Sacred Heart, a Catholic religious order. I was privileged to be an invited guest at their Australian chapter meeting. Twice I was conscious that some perfectly logical comments I made were offensive to "relational" sensibilities. They were the two I knew about. There can be as much separating "rational" and "relational" people as separates Catholics and Protestants! "Relational" people are concerned with relationships and how others perceive them. They are concerned with dignity and esteem. So spiritual "dryness" comes in situations where these are absent. There are many situations like this in our times, such as marital and family breakdown, work lay-offs, and other monetary setbacks that can create a spiritual desert for relational people.

Divine love, forgiveness, and acceptance are qualities of a relationship with Jesus and God that can be a powerful offering of Spirit to "relational" people. Spirit is God honoring that relationship and all our relationships. In our church, we often used the text, "For where two or three are gathered in my name, I am there among them," to excuse the fact of not as many people turning up for a function as we expected, or hoped for. There is more to it than that excuse. If we look at the extended text, we see that it pertains to relationships and offering forgiveness:

> Truly I tell you, whatever you bind on earth will be bound in heaven, and whatever you loose on earth will be loosed in heaven. Again, truly I tell you, if two of you agree on earth about anything you ask, it will be done for you by my Father in heaven. For where two or three are gathered in my name, I am there among them." (Matt. 18:18-20)

Out of the two obvious ways of reading the first line of this text, "relational" people tend to take it as a warning against leaving people bound in sin when time is running out, in contrast to seeing it as a power play about deciding who is bound and who is freed. They are concerned about people. The Spirit of Jesus in the midst of them is about caring relationships.

"Experiential" people are people of action. They are much more likely to say, "I feel," "I am touched," or "I am moved," than, "I think," when expressing an opinion. They are often the more intuitive and creative people in the neighborhood. If "rational" is a predominant characteristic of the modern epoch, then "experiential" can be identified with the period that preceded it. So the scientific, rationalist push has been damaging to this kind of personality. They sometimes have to mask it for the sake of their career. They make up the larger part of any alternative lifestyle people in the neighborhood. Therefore, their "dryness" comes from always having to "explain" himself or herself as someone more than a person to be experienced.

"Experiential" people are more at home with Spirit. For them, Spirit is immanent and transcendent—familiar and awesome! Spirit brings inner peace. Spirit gives a holistic dimension to life. As in Genesis 1:1, Spirit is creativeness hovering over chaos. Spirit initiates and leads towards action, and as the other side of this, Spirit is also stillness, silence, and a turning away from scientific observation to aesthetic appreciation.

"Character" zoning and Spirit

"Character" zoning lies between psychosocial zoning and demographic zoning with respect to Spirit. Character is related to lifestyle. Young families wanting something of the solid and enduring qualities of the housing to rub off onto their lives may populate a neighborhood of older housing stock. They look to the past to give them a base to tackle the present and future. Of course, the housing is thoroughly renovated. There is the charm of the past coupled with the convenience of modern technology. Such a group will look for Spirit in the same way, to provide solid connection and grounding with the past with effectiveness for living today. Traditional worship, done well and focused on current issues, can be a means of finding Spirit for this group.

Housing estates with green fields may have a number of houses built to evoke a past style but have a different character. There is more of a pioneering character in such places, and Spirit is looked to nurture a sense of adventure, community building, and, perhaps, counteract isolation and loneliness. It is hard to maintain this character once the housing estate (subdivision) has settled, but something of its more outgoing and mutually supporting character can be fostered for the next generation of residents. In a similar way, vestiges of 1970s hippie culture can create a "character" zone where Spirit nurtures a sense of justice and peacemaking. The corporate culture of a single, large employer or a military base in an area will also affect its character and hence the way Spirit is sought and made available.

Sometimes character will reflect a moral stance which Spirit helps support in the face of peer pressures and difficulty. Two families can live side by side in identical circumstances. One keeps family together and "straight," the other falls apart. Often the only difference is that one has engaged with Spirit through a local church and the other has not. Spirit has the power to break dependency and addiction.

National character is also at work. Australians, Americans, Canadians, and others may well approach their search and discovery of Spirit with a different nuance on otherwise similar circumstances because of their national character.

At Prospect Road we identified the characters of our neighborhoods and related them to the historical ministry gifts of the different centres of our multi-campus church—another kind of character—to help nuance our spirituality, but the primary response was to the psychosocial zoning. We have an "up-tempo" reworking of "rational" spirituality in two centres, "relational" spirituality in two, and "experiential" in the fifth centre. It is hard to imagine a declining local church as a place where people would come to engage with Spirit, because so much of what people would find there seems antithetical to Spirit. Often, however, a church's reputation lingers on in the neighborhood beyond the point where it is supported by reality. If the church has turned around to meet its times, its past character as a spiritual entity will be a "color" that adds to its energy and focus. The church's reputation will be confirmed by an experience of Spirit that matches the group's search.

Demographic zoning and Spirit

Demographic zoning allows fine-tuning in the offer of Spirit. Age distribution gives some sense of the way Spirit might be needed. At Prospect Road we confirmed the low numbers of baby-boomers and their teen-age and young adult offspring. We have a cohort of persons over sixty and another less than forty years of age. For the older people, spiritual dryness can be "rational" because of difficulty keeping up with the changes. It can also be a kind of nihilism and diminishing hope as future options start to narrow. For Gen-Xers with young families, spiritual dryness may be more relational. One young parent in our Parent/Child worship strand said, "This is quality family time," thus revealing an area of spiritual dryness for her and many like her. The moral character of the environment in which children will grow can also be an area of anxiety in which Spirit is seen as help. Suicide is the major cause of death among young males in Australia, indicating another area for which Spirit could be a helpful influence.

An analysis of education attainment levels can indicate "rational" and "relational" needs. A high level of educational attainment indicates a grouping that has been strongly influenced by the anti-religion, anti-Church attitudes in education[28] and professional life and hence has "rational" spiritual needs. Lower educational attainment levels may indicate "relational" spiritual needs. One scarcely needs demographic data to be aware of low and high social status areas, although newspapers sometimes list the "top" suburbs.

Ethnic groupings have special needs. Denominational groupings may give a sense of the character of an area, but the numbers should not be seen as either an encouragement or discouragement for Spirit, at least, not in Australia, where the biggest and fastest-growing denomination, is "no religion," and where actual affiliation is low. It is best to use the broad general needs for Spirit than to focus too much on denomination. Housing, employment, and other data will usually only confirm what can be observed.

OPEN GATES TO SPIRITUAL ENGAGEMENT

When I came to Prospect Road, one of the centres had been distributing a brochure that said, "The Doors of the Church Are Always Open." As a *modern* church, they had supposed that what was inside the doors was interesting and important enough to risk entering. This presupposition is not true for postmodern people. A postmodern church needs to consider,

What its target groups think might lie inside the door,
Where their spiritual search might be leading them, and
Whether the door of the church building is the best point
to engage.

The metaphor Open Gate refers back to the sheep farm from the Prologue. On the farm, when the sheep ran out of feed where they were grazing, the open gate allowed them to pass through to new grass and water. The sheep found the open gate and were free to wander in. They were not herded through it. An Open Gate implies a decision. "Will I enter or not?" To get a "Yes!" in response, there will need to be a realistic hope of finding Spirit on the other side of the gate.

In the past, a decision to give one's life to Jesus was both the beginning point and often the end point of spiritual journeying. Now postmoderns make and remake decisions as the journey proceeds and circumstances and experience impinge on faith and belief. The five Open Gates are described below as points of first entry to where a person might hope to engage with Spirit. The Open Gates are not incremental or hierarchical, contrary to our modern concept of growth. Any gate can be a beginning entry point. More than one gate will need to be entered to grow a full spiritual life in a person. At Prospect Road, we have had, so far, two people who have entered through the leadership gate without any prior faith relationship and only rudimentary knowledge and understanding of Jesus. They brought leadership skills and indigenous cultural awareness that we desperately needed as a church. There was an exchange—a shared pedagogy—in their growth. One went to worship, companionship, and Jesus as higher stages but is not yet into discipleship. The other has just begun and is headed into Jesus. She is the precious, first one of her generation in that community, so companionship might be further down the road. Discipleship and worship might be next for her. Both people are a gift of God to us. With God, we can work to provide what is needed in a timely way, but not necessarily in the conventional order. But unlike the past, the search for Spirit involves more than one entry point and time. A person may go through the gates several times at different decisional points and stages of spiritual maturity in life and find greener pastures of Spirit on the other side.

The gate that opens onto Spirit companionship

In a world where views are so strongly colored by scientific rationalism, a person's sense of, and curiosity about Spirit, feels strange. (Yearning for Spirit might be too strong a term.) With whom can they share these feelings, satisfy their curiosity, and explore Spirit a little deeper? Fronting up at the local church on Sunday is too "full on" for a person with these first stirrings of Spirit to be comfortable. People in the church are likely to expect a fuller understanding and experience of Spirit than the rather vague stirrings that they have. The Open Gate to Spirit companionship describes ways a small local church might employ to engage with these people at the stage they are at on their spiritual journey.

Such a person is looking for a one-on-one relationship with a person who is more familiar and confident with Spirit than they are, someone who is open and accessible enough to them that they can grow trust to the point where they can explore Spirit with them without feeling too awkward or embarrassed. They are looking for a Spirit companion. They are looking for someone to accompany them on their journey of exploration.

There is a caveat here for church people. In Christendom (the worldview of the church in the modern era), most persons in local churches came to Jesus as a stage of growing up. Persons were led to Christ through heightened emotions, convincing preaching, and having an experience of Christ that was considered normal and expected. As we move further into postmodernism, this approach will be counterproductive. What is required is not leading, where the church sets the agenda for finding Spirit, but accompanying, where the person sets the agenda.

What kinds of events or activities might open up Spirit companionship relationships? How might a person be accompanied to Spirit? Each local church will nuance its activities, according to the makeup of its target groupings and the leadership gifts available to it. What they might see, concretely, at Prospect Road, on the other side of this Open Gate are the following:

- Small groups with an open mix of churchgoers and non-churchgoers involved in something not overtly religious but that reflects the personal and social values of engaging with Spirit, e.g. coffee mornings at Neighborlink, play groups at Parentlink and Neighborlink, Parent/child/family events at Parentlink. Neighborlink is Prospect Road's outreach community for "relational" people and also for alienated and isolated people. Parentlink is the outreach community for "rational" people and also for parents and children.

- Personal pastoral contacts with key leaders.

- Meeting with "church people" involved in events as part of a non-church neighborhood network, e.g. the Primary School Parents and Friends.

The gate that opens onto worship

Worship is the most obvious Open Gate because of its accessibility. Service times are on every centre's notice board. Worship is a way of signifying one's journey with Jesus through drama, symbols, story, music, and the senses. A person looks through the Open Gate seeking experiences of Spirit through participating and engaging his or her senses in the drama, symbols, story and music of worship, and also observing how other people participating are affected. Participation rather than attendance is importance because it provides the searcher with an opportunity to contribute as well as receive, and to take a role in the Spirit encounter of others. Worship in which worshippers are passive recipients will be a less effective vehicle for Spirit in our times.

What they might see, concretely, at Prospect Road, on the other side of this Open Gate are the following:

- Four Way Worship is a service where four different strands of worship—Classic, Parent/Child, Discussion and Soul Café—run concurrently, weaving in and out of Classic Worship.

- Talk Back Worship is a service over a meal where people join in discussion, questions, and testimony in response to interviews, topical discussion, scriptural discussion, and praise.

- Learnerlink Worship is a simple, lay-led service in the classic mould with people sharing insights from Learnerlink courses.

- Spirit Workshop is a mealtime, small-group service that constructs contemplative installations, creates prayers, poems, and songs, and devises movements. It borrows from classic spirituality and popular culture and uses a flexible space with multimedia projection and hi-fi sound.

The gate that opens onto Jesus

In countries that in modern times considered themselves Christian, there remains a heritage that relates Spirit to Jesus. It has been seriously compromised in postmodern eyes by the assault on religion by scientific rationalism and by antipathy to the Church as an authoritarian structure. But once people have admitted the reality of Spirit to themselves, Jesus is a logical place to look for deepening Spirit in one's being. "Church" remains a stumbling block. In its Christendom form, Church can actually be counterproductive to finding Jesus in a way that that builds an encounter with Spirit by trying to bind people to a "Do as you're told" ideology. Such churches can end up with a different kind of modernism—religious tribalism, which in its more fanatical form is destructive and divisive.

Rather than "belonging to Jesus" in an institutional way, this search for Spirit focuses on a relationship with Jesus as a companion on the journey. Jesus is a metaphysical Spirit companion who accompanies in a similar way to the human Spirit companion at the first gate. However, here the trust has to be established between the searcher and the church, because his or her memory of Jesus is attached to "Church." Trust is built out of safe and affirming experiences. A first step in this journey is to break with the predominant anti-religion, anti-Church culture of our time. Trust will grow as questions are received openly and seriously, as questions to be worked through in an non-prescribed way. Trust will grow in the absence of any attempt to "capture" the searcher. Offering a choice of short-term, "Jesus encounters" helps assure the searcher that he or she is in control of the search.

How might the Spirit of Jesus accompany a person? Again, each congregation will nuance its activities, according to the makeup of their target groupings and the leadership gifts available. What they might see, concretely, at Prospect Road, on the other side of this Open Gate are the following:

- Short-term courses by Learnerlink on provocative topics that offer personal access to Spirit, Jesus, and Scripture in an open-ended way. Learnerlink is an outreach community primarily to "rational" people but has recently developed a different approach for outreach to "relational" people.

- An Alpha course.

- Soul Circuit—personal spiritual reflection and self-directed exploration of Spirit at Innerlink. Innerlink is an outreach community to "experiential" people, to youth and young adults.

The gate that opens onto discipleship

People look through the Open Gate to discipleship with the understanding that their search for Spirit is going to be a life-long quest. So they look for engagement with Spirit that is holistic, progressively more engaging and with an ongoing and deepening relationship to the other key elements in their life, like vocation, work, and family. In discipleship, people grow to understand how they too can be Spirit companions to others out of a deepening companionship with Jesus. This sounds like a subsequent stage to entry through one of the previous gates, and so it can be, but discipleship may also be a powerful dawning realization of the worth of Spirit encounter. If so, companionship with other Spirit seekers and with Jesus and participation in worship will quickly follow the first few nibbles on the other side of the Open Gate to discipleship. What could be most damaging to this search would be to discover that what was being offered was a Christendom model of discipleship—a catechism of right answers and a sense of expectation of "doing one's duty," rather than a posing of questions and a calling to serve.

What they might see, concretely, at Prospect Road, on the other side of this Open Gate are one or more of the following:

- Opportunities to expand and deepen understanding of the Bible using approaches to learning appropriate to the target groupings.

- Encouragement to take initiative and to identify and use personal gifts to serve others.

The gate that opens onto leadership

Leadership is not an expected beginning point for a search for Spirit, but, historically, for women and disadvantaged people the Church has been one of the few places where there was a way to access and learn leadership skills. The Church and trade unions were often the only places where people without money or influence could find the support and encouragement to get ahead.

Women's Fellowships (or Women's Circles) and Guilds opened up leadership to women, as did Property Committees (or Trustee Committees) to men.

We usually imagine that church leaders need to be committed and have a mature faith. There are two reasons why this may be considered differently. First, in a Church transitioning from Christendom to our present times, leaders may be committed but completely out of touch with the mission target group. To develop indigenous leaders, some people with grounding in local culture need to be encouraged with their first steps on a faith journey, and grow their faith and their leadership ability at the same time. Their relevance to the mission field has priority over orthodoxy or heredity. Second, we may be missing what God is bringing forward in that person's life. A person looks through the Open Gate to leadership and seeks ways to realize more of her or his potential by being engaged with Spirit. How this may be achieved will be looked at in greater detail later.

What they might see, concretely, at Prospect Road, on the other side of this Open Gate, are the following:

- Having initiative received positively with permission to act.

- Receiving mentoring and other encouragement and training to exercise leadership.

- Being enabled to be an agent of change and growth in oneself, the neighborhood, and the church.

This chapter has looked at Spirit as a generic word (just as God is a generic word) for the object of spiritual search and faith development. For small Christian churches, and large ones too, the object of spiritual search and faith development is Jesus. My purpose in being less overt about Jesus in this chapter is to help us enter the viewpoint of the Spirit seeker. In Australia, and probably in many other parts of the world as well, a Gen-X seeker's family may have had no contact with religion for two or three generations. We realize that at the point of the first step through one of the Open Gates, theology or doctrine or any of the church's attitudes to Jesus are irrelevant. Later, these introductions help people to make sense of their search for Spirit and their relationship to Jesus, or to expand and deepen it, and to appreciate the teaching that has given the church in which they now feel accepted its character.

---

[27] 1 Corinthians 9:22.

[28] Huston Smith, *Why Religion Matters*, p. 79ff. See Chapter 5 and particularly p. 101, "The New Professionalism." This is about the influence of American education on professional people, but it is equally true of education in Australia.

CHAPTER 4

Network Relationships

CREATING A NETWORK

When Robert, on his sheep farm, opened all the gates in times of drought and difficulty, he provided a choice of pasture and watering places for the sheep. He created a farm that was a network of pasture and watering places that changed the farm's character. With openness and choice, the reduced flock of breeding ewes and prize rams actually thrived rather than survived. Not only was the environment not degraded, but when better conditions eventually came, the countryside, the flock, and the whole farm enterprise were able to respond and increase its capacity easily and quickly.

At Prospect Road, we have created a church that is a network of spiritual "watering places" and mission outreach "pastures" to, first, enable the church to counter the hostility of scientific rationalism and to thrive in difficult times. But also, by responding sensitively and responsively to the cultural setting of our ministry, we will be well placed to respond with vigor to the emerging cultural paradigm of our times, as it becomes more widely accepted.

William Easum and Thomas Bandy used the metaphor of the Spiritual Redwoods to look at the nature and functioning of a church that is poised to thrive in this unfolding new era. In Chapter (Vista) Five of *Growing Spiritual Redwoods* they discuss the way that church relationships flow.[29] They use the word *inclina-*

tion to discuss the way that this flow develops. Networks are one of three "inclinations" of Spiritual Redwoods.[30]

Recently, the European Union commissioned research into ways of linking universities, industry, and government into innovation networks. North American and Japanese cultures have been working on this type of convergence for many years to grow their economies. The SEIN project's focus is on the structure and dynamics of networks.[31] One of the project papers, by Günter Küppers of the University of Bielefeld in Germany, gives helpful insights that have extended my understanding of Easum and Bandy and my praxis at Prospect Road.[32] Like Easum and Bandy, Küppers recognizes that networks are a new form of social relationship that has emerged in response to social change.

> "In recent decades, society has witnessed the development of a new form of coordinating social activities which falls beyond that of traditional formal markets and organizations. In scientific literature, this phenomenon is referred to as a network, a concept that is not necessarily easy to define. Within the social sciences, it is used whenever social interaction transcends individual social structures (such as groups, organizations, systems) but is nevertheless perceived as representing a clearly distinguishable form of social integration. Clearly defined boundaries—particularly organizational boundaries—are not a prerequisite for networks. Given that a variety of actors may be involved in a network at different points in time, it is also not possible to talk about this form of social integration as having some kind of center or core."[33]

The emergence of the network is also consistent with the insight of John Walsh, describing the social paradigm shift of our time as a move from "Do as you're told!" to a "Do it yourself!" attitude that increasingly finds hierarchical institutions and contractual obligations personally restrictive.[34]

Uncertainty

Küppers explains this change of view in terms of different ways of dealing with uncertainty. In his view, organizations exist to reduce uncertainty to manageable levels. In general, organizations try to eliminate uncertainty by rules, regulations, and procedures or, in the case of markets, by contracts and exchange rates. Retrospectivity also reduces uncertainty. Most rules and regulations are derived from common law—the codifying of experience. A closer examination shows that uncertainty can never actually be completely eliminated. Complexity always introduces uncertainty to any situation.

With networks, knowing what to do in a situation comes from reflecting on experience but not in the "We tried it once and it didn't work" kind of way often used to stifle initiative. Networks rely on ongoing and repeated action/reflection in what Küppers calls circular causality. In that process, "We tried it once and it didn't work" becomes an opportunity to refine what was done and to experiment with different ways of getting a better outcome. Instead of being prepared to live with failure, the failure becomes an indication that whatever it was that needed to be fixed by the projected action is still there as a troubling and disturbing "thorn." With organizations, "the buck" stops with whoever is in charge. With markets, it is whoever signs the contract, but with networks it is whoever can discern a way forward. Such discernment might need an expanded viewpoint to see new factors that need to be taken into account or wider implications that need to be considered. A change of outcome might only need a small change of action or a complete revamp. Küppers' paper goes on to refine this loop of circular causality to describe how networks work to allow different entities—in his case, business, government and universities—their different viewpoints, perspectives, and expertise, which make identifying the factors needed to achieve innovative outcomes more probable. At Prospect Road, four mission outreach teams with different viewpoints, perspectives, and expertise on mission are, in a similar way, achieving a breakthrough in mission that the five previous, organizationally bound congregations could not.

There are two key interfaces for networks. One is the interface with the task. Most of this book is about that. The other is the interface with the other two forms of getting things done: organizations and markets. For small churches, this includes relating to denominational structures, civic ordinances, and other churches, to name a few. Some small churches, particularly house churches and independent churches, minimize these relationships, but for mainstream churches in the process of transformation, such as Prospect Road, need to consider how this interface works. At Prospect Road, the Church Council is our network/organization interface, and networking is one of its major roles.

Transforming a church from an organization to a network means finding ways of breaking free from the "certainty" of institutional behavior to commence local interactions to set up circular causality. One of these ways I have mentioned earlier. Research into the "edge of chaos" has shown that increasing complexity to a level between a stable state and a chaotic state of being increases the "fitness" of the organization to function in its environment. Increasing complexity implies an increase in uncertainty. Three or four options and choices of how one should act or where one should engage is very much "Do it yourself." In part, therefore, the changing culture is conditioning us to sit more comfortably with being uncomfortable. The recently released 2001 Australian census results have been greeted with headlines of "We're a nation of independents" and "Life at 40: more comfort, less ease." Similar findings would be repeated around the Western world.

Faith and uncertainty

Acting in faith is another way of acting out of uncertainty. With faith, uncertainty in this world is countered with a certainty about God. Faith trusts that God calls, guides, leads, encourages, and fulfils human endeavor. When people act in faith, they act in their own best judgment of God's calling, guiding, leading, and encouragement. This action occurs in the concrete reality of their life situation in order to participate with God in a global structure that fulfils God's vision and purpose. Faith takes the Church into circular causality. It remains an action undertaken in uncertainty, because each reflection on what happens when the church acts in faith reveals new but unclear glimpses of God's leading.

When faith is codified, it becomes religion. Religion acts counter to faith throughout both Old Testament and New Testament Scripture. The struggle between the "fleshpots of Egypt" and the uncertainties of the journey to the Promised Land is echoed in the stories about people of faith and stories of idol worship throughout the history of Israel. In Romans 4:13-25, Paul contrasts the faith of Abraham with the religion of obedience to the Law and points out that "removing" certainty by religion empties faith of meaning. Uncertainty is inherent to faith.

The struggle between religion and faith is a potent issue in most small congregations. As their uncertainty increases because of changes in demography, or their own aging, or a hostile mission field, or any of the other attitudinal changes of the emerging era, then religion becomes dominant. Religion is living on the memory of the glory days of the church, or in comfortable patterns of controlling individuals and groups, or in disengagement from the mission field. This kind of religion makes it difficult for both the congregation and those leaders with vision trying to transform and enliven their ministry. Often congregations like these feel written off by the wider Church, being seen as basket cases for church growth by the movers and shakers of the denomination. But as long as they are placed in a center of population, they can be effective mission outposts in a postmodern mission field. The clue is to discern, claim, and grow their gifts for the situation, however dormant they may be, rather than be intimidated by the (more obvious) problems.

At Prospect Road, there was no way that the worshipers at the Islington Centre were going to change. They were the oldest foundation in Prospect Road Uniting Church, dating back to the 1840s. Their origins were in the Primitive Methodist tradition. All the other centres were part of the Wesleyan Methodist tradition. They had been "the runt of the litter" in former Methodist church clusters, and now they felt imposed upon again. Some hoped they would be dead before the church changed. Others did all the things that "opposition to change" people do: boycotts, complaints to denominational authorities, and personal denigration of the change agents. This went on for five years, and then they came on board with the changes. Now they show an excitement and engagement in mission that is an example to some of those who were the earliest to say, "Yes!"

The beginning point for creating a network church for the twenty-first century is to strengthen faith: Help people to find their certainty in God and to loosen their dependence on the much more fragile "certainties" of the institution. Prayer and spiritual discernment are critical. We prayed and talked and sought God's leading for over six months before we took the initial action that became the causal loop of action and reflection that has made Prospect Road a self-organizing innovation network that is growing in spiritual energy, effectiveness, and numbers. We emphasized the fragility and foolishness of trying to maintain the status quo, and we confronted the suicidal impulses to find certainty in death by calling for God's vindication and fulfillment of all the years of loyal service and mission endeavor that had been carried out over the past thirty years, without any sign of it succeeding. We discovered and began to live in response to our spiritual DNA rather than the institution, or to the "comfort zones" of the church centres from which Prospect Road was formed, with their cliques and controllers, or to a fatalistic attitude of waiting for death.

COMMUNICATION

The first church where I served as pastor was a collection of four small, rural churches. Church board meetings were held fairly infrequently, because of distance and bad roads, and were at my home. The meetings were usually brief, because there was a general reticence to speak. Business over, there was a shared supper, and then the real meeting started. Over the next hour or so, the meeting agenda was revisited with animated discussion and wise conclusions. No longer constrained by structure, the board members could "be themselves," and in that mode they did good work.

The "real meeting" is the mode of communication for networks in contrast to hierarchical orders, instructions, and briefings or market contracts.[35] As demonstrated in my experience years ago, open communication is needed to maintain network vitality and effectiveness. However, it took nearly forty years before I actually applied what I learned then. In between, I was molded by rules of meeting procedure set down by the Church and the expectations of local church leaders about how the business of the church should be negotiated. But as Prospect Road has developed into a network church, so the mode of communication has developed too.

Agendas have been changed to give the highest priority and greatest time to the key mission issues of each team, with the clutter of routine issues relegated to the last part of the meeting. The agenda is a powerful symbol. A more recent development for one team has eliminated reports from the agenda. The agenda is divided into two sections: core issues and non-core issues. Issues are aired, and decisions and actions agreed in an open forum for each section. At the end of each forum, the decisions are framed into formal motions and minutes. This format reduces any sense of hierarchical control that may still be lurking.

At Prospect Road, communication is opened up to the whole church constituency by making most meeting decisions and information transparent to general view and informal discussion. A climate of trust has been fostered and maintained. This ability to "know" turns the "scuttlebutt" of small congregation life into a form of "communication-through-discussion." An informal ministry also promotes this sense of openness, transparency, and non-institutional, and discursive communication "by walking around." Once again the setting can say much. Meeting someone in a coffee shop on Main Street is a "communication-through-discussion" setting that conveys something quite different from the hierarchical implications of a meeting across a desk or even across a coffee table in an office. But the "communication-through-discussion" has to happen in a consistent way through all the congregation's meetings in order for network relationships to assist the process of transforming a church to be missionally effective in the emerging era.

MINIMIZING CONTROL

Control is the antithesis of "communication-through-discussion." Control is the communication mechanism of line management, and networks cannot function with this form of communication. Furthermore, control, because it limits options for actions to those approved by the controlling person, group or committee, is a major stumbling block for mission outreach in a "do it yourself" era.

Most churches are over-controlled. Committees report to committees which report to the church board, which reports to denominational authorities in their many-layered bureaucracy. This is particularly disastrous for small churches as key people's time and energy is diverted from extending the missional outreach of the church to propping up its structure. Further, these committees are a direct cause of burnout and "drop out" in small churches, because so much committee work is empty of meaning, unproductive, and so hard to stand down from that it becomes a kind of life sentence. As the church faces the crises of our times, restructuring has tried to reduce the number of levels of reporting, but line management and control prevail. "Permission giving" is another restructuring strategy in line management that tries to minimizes control.

Tom Bandy in *Christian Chaos—Revolutionizing the Congregation* has developed a servant-empowering model of management. In it he differentiates between prescriptive thinking and proscriptive thinking.

"Prescriptive thinking lists everything that a committee, program or church office *can or should do.* It prescribes activity in the same way a doctor prescribes medicine for a patient. Proscriptive thinking defines the boundaries beyond which a ministry team, program, or church leader *cannot go, but within which they are free to take initiative.*"[36]

Minimizing prescriptive thinking and maximizing proscriptive thinking is a way of minimizing control.

Bandy relates these two forms of thinking with accountability and productivity, building a comprehensive picture of a thriving church. He does so with regard to the general institutional form of church. Small churches and network churches will benefit from Bandy's insights, but may need to adjust them. For example, at Prospect Road we have reduced the role of the congregation meeting to that of giving formal approval or disapproval of the stated consensus from specially convened open congregational workshops. This acts in the same way as the congregation meeting in Bandy's model. Small churches can build in a high degree of general awareness and involvement that is lost in larger churches where it is physically impossible to know "Who's who" and "What's what."[37] By implementing the workshop or open forum rather than a "members only" meeting, the whole congregation is coached in its "being-for-mission" (or DNA), and this fosters the attitudinal changes to church life that further reduce the power and influence of control mechanisms and promote the change from organization to network.

Bandy's book includes a helpful section on small-church relationships and the arrangements that can be made to improve effectiveness.[38] Amalgamation is one suggestion. Amalgamation at Prospect Road has certainly been effective, although we have given it our own spin by not rationalizing the properties in the process. The advantages of this have been noted elsewhere, but there have been two advantages for minimizing control. Amalgamating to become a single congregation (with four outreach communities) has simplified both internal relationships and external denominational relationships and their attendant bias to control. Amalgamation has also upset the spheres of influence of controllers, making them more vulnerable to change and abolition.

There is no hierarchy with networks, which is why control as a characteristic of hierarchy is so much out of place. Where prescriptive thinking is required because of accountability or the denominational rulebook, its exercise needs careful consideration. At Prospect Road we deal with it in two ways. First, we have set up our church council (board) to act as a bulwark between external institutional bodies with their prescriptive thinking and the church network, and, second, we have considered that the prescriptive responsibilities of the church council toward the teams in the church network are "reserved" powers. That is, they are there, but only exercised when absolutely necessary, to resolve a dispute or impasse. In general, when the proscriptive boundaries are well known, righteousness is fulfilled without having to be demanded.

Because control—the structures that encourage prescriptive thinking—and controllers—the people who have found personal power through those structures—can have a devastating effect on postmodern mission and change and in particular on network relationships, there is a growing body of literature on how best to deal with both phenomena. For the leaders of a church being transformed it can be a frustrating and time-consuming, but necessary, work. Prospect Road brought together five small declining churches in which control was endemic and controllers benignly ruled little empires.

Leadership needs to model proscriptive thinking. It is alarming to realize how much control lurks in one's own psyche. Every time control shows, it needs to be a point for growth in the leader's faith, vision of the mission, and servant-empowering role. It comes up within me through the "imperialism" of my own ideas. It is necessary to go strongly for what one sees as the necessary initiative but not to bulldoze other people's questioning of it. When I am faithful, I am able to hand over the idea to God and to listen to what God is saying in other people's critique, secure in the knowledge that if this idea fails to grow legs, God will provide another one, often out of the very situation in which I have found myself hard pressed. One's strong points and weak points show up together. For me it is ideas, for another it will be relationships, for another feelings. For each of us, our strengths and weaknesses should lead us to God and God's purposes rather than power and our own purposes.

TALKING THE TALK AND WALKING THE WALK

The purpose of relationships in a network church is to bring people into a relationship with Jesus Christ. *Spirit* is the beginning and end point of the process. *Skill* is what it takes to communicate effectively and reflect on its outcomes. *Situation* is the particular cultural setting where the praxis of gospel sharing takes place. In Küppers' model of circular causality in networks, and in particular his development of it with respect to innovation networks,[39] construction of meaning and generation of new hypotheses move to design of experiments and generation of effects which move to observation of effects, integration of data, and back to construction of meaning. Then circular causality repeats, building on the experience gained.

The causal loop of mission outreach is more complex than Küppers' scientific model, but considering it in this way helps create a culture of outreach in the church. I suggest that the mission outreach causal loop functions like a "low" in climate change. The "mission outreach" of the low-pressure system is to bring rain to refresh the land. Working in a clockwise direction (in the Southern Hemisphere; counter-clockwise in the Northern Hemisphere), the dry winds off the land gather moisture as they move out over the ocean. Somewhere in the loop, clouds form and then build up into a storm front. The temperature drops behind the front and the rain falls.

Church leaders can use meteorology as a metaphor. The starting point is the Spirit of the church and its desire to find effective ways of communicating the gospel to people. This "ocean depth" of Spirit adds more and more Spirit to the dry winds of unbelief and spiritual yearning coming from the mission field. This increase of Spirit coalesces into a vision for action, which then builds to a "storm front" of effectiveness that "pours" Spirit on the mission field through evangelism and service. In the rainy season, one low follows another, so that the cycle is repeated, but beginning from a "wetter" starting point, until the land is saturated with rain. So each part of the loop builds and grows with each cycle of circular causality, increasing the effectiveness of the evangelism and service. Of course, there is a point where the metaphor breaks down. The floods that come from an excess of rain are a doubtful benefit to the land-based people, but a flood of Spirit would be something else!

Figure 1 sets out the components of circular causality for mission outreach, and the meteorological metaphor implies something of the variability and volatility of the process. It sets out the broad parameters of a process that works in a different way than line management decision-making. Jesus used the procreative cycle as his "circular causality" metaphor when he spoke to Nicodemus in John 3, but he countered any cause and effect conclusions that Nicodemus might draw with a weather metaphor, "The wind blows where it chooses, and you hear the sound of it, but you do not know where it comes from or where it goes. So it is with everyone who is born of the Spirit." Jesus' qualification is already built into our weather map metaphor, especially as the "storm front" builds through "Leadership Discernment & Growth" and "Team Deployment."

Figure 1. The meteorological metaphor of circular causality for mission outreach (*weather map courtesy of the Australian Bureau of Meteorology*).

Situation: relating to the area

To create and maintain a causal loop for mission outreach requires *Spirit* and a relationship to faith, *Skill* and a relationship to task, *Situation* and a relationship to the mission field. Spirit always initiates Mission, but I suggest that the process should start by developing a relationship to the mission field. Küppers observes, "A new scientific theory remains meaningless unless its author can convince the scientific community that it is capable of solving an important scientific question. An innovation must function properly, it must fit into a specific social praxis."[40]

Some years ago our denominational authorities, alarmed by decline, commissioned a major statewide consultation to plan for renewal. After two years the project finished, having made insignificant inroads into the problem despite masses of planning. There was general enthusiasm for the program and some minor cosmetic changes but no praxis. Perhaps, as Bandy says,

> "It is not that declining church organizations ignore productivity completely. They simply limit productivity dramatically. The actual mission opportunities seized by the organization are few, but the supervision and management of those few mission opportunities involve the intensive involvement of many, many congregational participants."[41]

Perhaps these efforts are stymied by a theology of two realms or kingdoms: This theology holds that what happens in the world from Monday to Saturday must be kept separate from what happens in church on Sunday. Whatever the reason, it makes sense to engage with one's area in order to identify and begin to relate to the people to whom the church hopes to minister. At least some preliminary answers to this question are needed, "What is it about our experience of Jesus that the people in our area can't live without?"[42]

Demographic data can give an intellectual feel for the area, but walking and talking give a greater understanding of the data. Beauty parlors are good information nodes. Taking business to local firms and getting to know the proprietors and staff can provide opportunities for insightful information. Some people are good at chatting in supermarket queues and bus stops. Once outreach has begun, new participants can help reflect on what the church is doing. This preliminary engagement helps build confidence and contacts for later outreach relationship building.

Think broadly and inclusively about the extent of the mission area to be served. At Prospect Road we considered the total area served by the five centres and added some adjacent areas without churches with easy access to our ministry. While each centre has a focused target grouping, working on the larger area allows choice and covers demographic pockets that may not be attracted to their nearest centre. It is surprising how much "horse and buggy" or "walking distance" values are embedded in a church leader's thinking, especially where, like Prospect

Road, the pre-mission-launch congregation is elderly.

Part of our Prospect Road area contains a tract of public housing with two of our centres serving it. But over the years, the church grew away from its area, becoming a refuge for those who were or who saw themselves as "upwardly mobile." Attitudes of condescension and antipathy are major hurdles for the church to overcome. New leaders, who have a rapport with the area, were found on the margins of the church and "brought up higher." It is essential for a church to understand its situation in order to have effective, mission-centered, outreach praxis.

Spirit: relating to faith

Spirit is the where each phase of circular causality for mission outreach begins. It is the ocean of Spirit that provides the impetus to move into uncertainty, and it does so by grounding our vision and intentions in the certainty of God's love in Jesus. We are convinced and strengthened in faith, in the same way as the apostle Paul, who said,

> For I am convinced that neither death, nor life, nor angels, nor rulers, nor things present, nor things to come, nor powers, nor height, nor depth, nor anything else in all creation will be able to separate us from the love of God in Christ Jesus our Lord.
> (Romans 8:38, 39)

It will take all of that conviction to face the uncertainty of mission outreach and engage in a faith-sharing relationship with the people God has given for ministry.

Prayer is the primary means of growing the church's faith, together with scriptural reflection on the heroes and heroines of Scripture who faced uncertainty with courage and determination and fulfilled their divine calling. Use the relationship that is beginning to form with the area as the context. Pray for groups, key people, offer their issues before God, and ask for discernment as to how the church might respond or how Jesus might satisfy their needs. Then pray for the visioning and mission planning processes of the church. At Prospect Road, we spent six months in fortnightly open meetings, alternating between visioning and planning and prayer. The breakthroughs at the planning meetings led to thanksgiving, the sticking points to requests for help. It is this interplay that grows a relationship to faith—to being able to "take off" into action where most things are uncertain. Finally, pray for leaders with the gifts and skills for the task to be called out to lead the church into mission praxis and to learn and grow from the consequences of their engagement. At Prospect Road, this aspect of prayer went beyond the initial six months, because it took time and "on the job" experience for the best available leaders to emerge.

Vision casting is almost as important as prayer in preparing a church to take the leap of faith into mission outreach. After six months, all we had at Prospect Road was:

1. That the five centres would amalgamate to form one congregation

2. That we would retain the five centres and replant worshipping communities in them, and

3. That the mission outreach and worship at each would be different and traditional worship would be centered on one site.

That was enough to trigger the circular causality that is transforming Prospect Road. It was a hard decision with many caveats in people's hearts but they did it. They did it, not seeing more than a glimpse of the future. They faced uncertainty because over the period of discernment they had come into a relationship with their faith. One of the questions that prescriptive thinkers ask about Prospect Road is, "Where else have you seen this working?" Only a few are able to see that, with Spirit, it is possible for a bunch of elderly Christian people to do something original and innovative.

Church leaders and members also need a motivating vision for change. For the modern era, the metaphor that has freighted the dominant motivating vision for New World cultures like Australia and North America has been "creating civilization from wilderness." This metaphor always included the church as one of the markers of civilization, along with the schoolhouse, law and order, and neat rows of picket-fenced houses. Current church growth strategies tend to work out of this metaphor. Most large churches in Australia started as church plants in green-fields housing developments. The metaphor of "creating civilization from wilderness" continues as these churches grow. It becomes a metaphor advancing civilization through churches that are large, diverse, fast-paced, and urbane, and that mirror the best of big-city living. None of this metaphor works in the established areas of towns and cities, even in areas of urban re-development. The infrastructure of civilization in these places is perceived as already in place.

In an established urban environment different metaphors are needed to motivate change. At Prospect Road an apocalyptic metaphor motivated change. It can be summed up as:

> **The old way is about to end.**
> **There is a way forward.**
> **We face a time of persecution and difficulty.**
> **Change to be part of the new reality now before it is**
>   **too late.**
> **God will vindicate the faithful.**

This message resonates with that of Jesus in his time. The practical expressions of this at Prospect Road were:

1. The announcement by the biggest church in the cluster that they were going to separate themselves from the cluster.

2. The appointment of a pastor with the gifts to lead the church forward.

3. Facing instead of ignoring the reality of a hostile mission field that had frustrated all the best efforts of the church over the past thirty years.

4. We had a five-year "window of opportunity" to do something different before people were too old and too few to do anything.

5. Those who had worked so hard to support and grow
   the church over the thirty years in the wilderness
   might glimpse "the Promised Land."

This motivating vision has worked, but it will not motivate future circular-causality cycles as Gen-Xers replace our older people.

This current generation is less and less likely to face a physical wilderness of raw countryside or housing development and more likely to face an existential wilderness of emptiness and meaninglessness. A line of dialogue from the movie, *The Fight Club*, sums it up.

> "If my culture, the West, all it provides me with is an apartment in a beautiful building stocked with Ikea furniture, and a meaningless job, and there is nothing else to believe in, then my life has become absurd."[43]

The new metaphor will come from the ecological movement. Something like the "sustainable development" that matches and considers the needs of the environment as well as the economy and considers the question, "What kind of world am I bequeathing to my grandchildren?" It will be a metaphor that is holistic. "Spirit" will be one of its markers, just like "megachurch" is the marker in the waning metaphor of "civilizing the wilderness."

Implementation and revision: relating to the task

The church relates to its task by identifying and equipping teams of people who will take the vision and the story and create ways to realize them, practically and effectively, in the mission area. At Prospect Road, we set up five teams, one for each of the four mission foci we had identified in our area plus the church council. If the little "Them, Those and Us" rural church I mentioned earlier ever got serious about its mission outreach it might join with other churches in its area to create a mission team for "them," a mission team for "those," a mission team for "us" and an "oversight" mission team to hold all the mission outreach together and keep the teams focused on the whole area.

The coordinating team needs special consideration. At Prospect Road we changed the church council from an administrative committee to an oversight mission team. In the process we had to change their notion of "oversight" from prescriptive thinking and control relationships to being the team, which with respect to the mission, is responsible for maintaining the "big picture" and the Spirit dynamic of the whole mission effort. We knew we had succeeded when one long-standing member finally stopped bringing the book of church regulations to meetings! The coordinating team exhorts the church, like the apostle Paul did in 1 Corinthians 12, to be the Body of Christ, honoring its parts and honoring their mutuality. But the coordinating team has an additional task as part of its "big picture" ministry—to include the denominational authorities and other external institutions in its view without allowing their prescriptive thinking to hobble the team's and the church's mission.

Initially, we allowed the old management committees to continue and created the new mission outreach teams in parallel, with some crossover membership. In God's good time, which was sooner rather than later, they gratefully and gracefully retired. Team members are discerned and invited to be part of the team. They remain in the team for as long as they continue to be effective. The church council formally recognizes the mission outreach teams. This formal recognition is part of the "bulwark" function of the church council. On the denominational-authority side of the bulwark, the teams look like committees of the church council. On the local mission side of the bulwark, they operate under a broad proscription that allows initiative and independence but links each part to the whole. Economic prudence is covered by regular audits, and church council and the denominational authorities handle major property development legalities. Each team is responsible for the worshiping and serving community related to its particular task and focus and has direct responsibility for the property and finance it needs.

Team members are selected by discernment of their gifts for the task. There are a number of qualities to look for. The first is affinity with the mission target group and area. The smartest, best-informed, and most spiritual team in the world is useless unless it can bring Jesus to the people in a way that they can understand and appreciate. Choosing members means discerning who can "walk the walk and talk the talk" with the people.

Another value for discerning team members is to recognize those who have caught the vision and who have "the heart of Jesus" for the people and the task. Appointment should be the confirmation of the call of God to the person to be a part of the team. Some assessment of their toughness for the task is also necessary. This kind of mission consciousness is what God showed Gideon when he needed to know who he should take with him to defeat the Midianites.[44]

Something of the audacity and originality of Gideon's tactics to win his battle needs to be reflected in the approach of mission outreach teams to their area and the task of bringing Jesus to the people. The skill phases of circular causality—designing and applying the praxis for mission outreach and evaluating and creating a new, revised praxis—need those qualities if the vision and prayed-for expectations of the church are to be successfully translated so that people respond. Similar skill is needed to evaluate what is being done and to so frame it for visioning and prayer that the church's ongoing efforts are even more effective and innovative.

For some years, churches have used spiritual gift inventories and other listings to match people with the right gifts and skills to the tasks of mission outreach. But there can be problems with lists like these. One of my contemporaries in younger days drew up a list of twenty or so attributes a wife needed to have. When he ultimately married, the marriage was a disaster! Fitting broad scriptural categories of gifts to specific mission purposes can be just as unreal. If we are going to argue for gift-based mission outreach teams, we need to have as much sense about "gifts" as we have developed about ministry.

With small churches the pool of people can be too small to find enough people with the right mix of gifts to form a team. Team members can be "grown" to improve their skills and effectiveness, so it is worth looking at the margins. Not everyone will come through, but encouragement, coaching, mentoring, and developing trust are good modeling behaviors for church leaders. Usually people respond.

What has been said about teams is even more important with respect to leaders. We are growing and fractalling new leaders from the people, but in an area with a growing number of young Gen-X families we had none in the church and none in sight. We needed a skilled Gen-X parent to help build a "critical mass" of young parents from whom growth and leadership can come. So we hired a young family worker for ten hours per week, and our work with young parents has begun to grow. Similar very part-time hiring will add youthful know-how to our learning center and our neighborhood relationships ministry.

A new organic metaphor, Companion Planting, describes cooperative relationships that Prospect Road has developed with two "outside" church groups. Gardeners know that some plants grow well together. While being quite different plant species, the presence of one next to the other enhances the well-being of both, e.g. tomatoes and basil. They also are complementary eaten together. Churches can work together locally in the same way. Prospect Road has developed two such relationships, one with Peter Kahrimanis, an independent Pentecostal evangelist and his Word of God Ministry. Peter's theology, ministry style, and practices are as "foreign" to the Uniting Church as ours are to him, yet the two ministries complement each other. The other relationship is with The Other Late, Late Service (TOLLS), which is an unincorporated, non-denominational group of young adults running radically alternative sensory worship.

Our "companion planting" relationships are mutually beneficial. On our part, because Prospect Road retained its five properties when the original churches amalgamated we have spaces that we can use in special ways without disrupting our own programs. So we have made space available free of charge for Peter's charismatic, evangelistic barbeques and rallies and, in another place, space for the alternative, sensory worship of TOLLS with its hi-fi sound, projection sails (screens), and in-the-round format.

On their part, the companion plantings enhance the mission of the church in the area. Peter reaches people on the margins of society and helps them get their lives together with love and Jesus, and TOLLS links us with young singles and students we would otherwise never reach.

They also fit in, in general, with our more open attitude towards denominational authority. Both groups are highly proscriptive. Even in quite involved cooperative activities, the independence of all parties is respected. There is also a non-competitive aspect. Each of the "companion plants" is an alternative, additional choice for those looking for Spirit. There is no obligation. Either party can walk away from the relationship at any time, although, because of the trust that has grown, such a step would be more painful in practice than the arrangement suggests.

In addition, each companion planting fits well with the mission emphasis of the centres where they are located: mission emphases based on our analysis of the areas served by those centres. So Peter's ministry involves relationship building, moderating social and family dysfunction and is focused strongly on love and Jesus. TOLLS ministry is alternative, challenging mainstream values, and is focused on an action-based but mystical relationship with Jesus similar to our own ministry purpose for that centre. Both relationships were initiated differently. Prospect Road "head-hunted" TOLLS, but Peter "head-hunted" Prospect Road.

If it is important that faith and vision get translated into praxis through the mission outreach teams, it is also important that the same teams evaluate the praxis and return to prayer and visioning for a new round of mission outreach, driven by circular causality. One could be tempted to think that, having done it once, there would be less uncertainty and more faith to initiate new mission outreach. But if the praxis failed, then doubt and uncertainty about taking another new initiative increase. Similarly, if the praxis goes well, the thought of moving from comparative certainty to uncertainty again is daunting. If having a good thesis without testing it in praxis is useless, then good praxis without refinement and change will gradually lose effectiveness and wither. For a few years, mid-career, I worked as a community arts officer for a local authority. During that time a British counterpart visited Australia for a series of workshops. One thing she said stuck, "Whenever I take on a project I keep one question at the back of my mind: 'What next?'" Achieving the "what next" always needs faith and vision. Change and complexity continue. Circular causality is always dynamic and if it becomes static, it breaks down. In fact, circular causality is a fractal—a pattern that shows up in a similar way at any level of the process and is used at every stage of the cycle—every time the mission is being considered. A fractal is a pattern in nature (and in computer representations of complexity) that repeats itself in every magnification or reduction of its being. Thus the brachiform pattern of a tree viewed as a whole is repeated in the root system, in the main branch formation, in smaller branches, in twigs and in the veins of the leaves.

GROWING LEADERS

One of the ways of turning prayer and vision into praxis is to consider "Who next?" Moses, at the end of his life, glimpsed the Promised Land. He knew that he would not make it, but he had made sure that a new leader, Joshua, would lead the people into it.[45] Part of the faith and vision stimulus that takes mission into circular-causality innovation is to find leaders to take one's place. Applying the organic metaphor of fractal to the church means that the pattern of leader-people relationships repeats itself from the pattern of the church overall to the pattern of its smallest group.

The relationship of members to teams, teams to communities, and communities to the congregation is a repeated organic fractal pattern. Wayne Cordeiro, lead pastor of New Hope Church in Hawaii, pioneered using fractals as a way of describing how teams work in his church. New Hope Church is a new church with church attendances of over 7,000. He describes his use of fractals and fractalling in his book, *Doing Church as a Team*.[46] The fractal pattern of New Hope Church works like this: Every leader has responsibility to grow and extend his or her mission responsibility. As the mission grows, the leader finds who will in turn extend the mission. The initiating leader then has to grow him or herself to provide the different kind of leadership required for the larger group of leaders and people. Over-extension of the leader's responsibility is prevented by limiting the span of responsibility to four people. This "extension" principle in fractalling that is present in Wayne Cordeiro's model needs to be present in any other model. It works in the same way as nature. The first leaf shoot extends to become a stem with many leaves and that extends to become a twig with many stems and so on. This aspect of New Hope's pattern is a fractal and fractals are organic.

In the diagrams that Cordeiro uses in his book to illustrate this process, the metaphor and symbols used are those of the line management organization. In my mind, such an organization would become very complex, cumbersome, and mechanistic, with something like seven tiers of management. New Hope's track record belies this risk. Perhaps networks and circular causality provide a more realistic metaphor for New Hope's leadership fractalling pattern.

If we follow the example of the church crèche that Cordeiro uses, then the crèche leader, using circular causality, researches the childcare needs of the church, reflects on needs, facilities, and best childcare praxis, as the context for prayer and a vision for childcare emerges. He or she then discerns and calls a team of people who implement a childcare program. Meanwhile, the church grows. There are more children and enough to have different programs for each age cohort. Once again the situation calls for reflection on needs, facilities, and best childcare praxis. Prayer and visioning discerns and calls new leaders who then discern and call new teams to handle the more specialized ministry. Meanwhile, the crèche leader now has a bigger, more complex situation on which to reflect. The new leaders and teams handle the details. The crèche leader's situation may now include discussion with the worship leader. Lack of crèche capacity may be becoming a block to the growth of the worship service. The context becomes broader and deeper. One of the earlier age cohort leaders may now be discerned and called as crèche leader as the former crèche leader begins working in his or her new context. Fractalling has happened in an organic and networked way rather than mechanistic and bureaucratic.

Without first-hand knowledge, I suspect this might be a better metaphor to describe the New Hope model.

As Prospect Road grows using New Hope's "extension" fractal, each new team that emerges will have a similar discerned and called relationship with the outreach teams for each community as the ministry grows. What is emerging is a matrix of relationships in which the least prominent are as important as the most prominent, rather than a hierarchy, much as St. Paul outlined with his "body" metaphor for the Church in 1 Corinthians 12:12 ff. and other places. Prospect Road is extending its leadership and teams through fractalling. However, unlike New Hope in Hawaii, Prospect Road in Australia is not a new church plant but a transformation of an existing church cluster. Our outreach and coordinating teams have been set up initially to grow the future church from a transformed past church.

The five main teams were brought into being through prayer and visioning workshops of the whole congregation and our major re-evaluations and new initiatives have come about in the same way. In turn, the teams have been called into being, through prayer and visioning with their communities. This is a "top down" prophetic and priestly role of discerning God's leading, calling, encouraging and blessing people and teams to initiate and support mission outreach tasks.

Figure 2. The action/reflection fractal of circular causality for mission outreach.

There is a fractal, crossover loop of circular causality that exists at every point and every level and cycle of the process illustrated in Figure 2. This loop suggests that the Spirit Node, as the faith-engendering function that empowers us to face uncertainty, must be active in everything that any church, Christian leader or team does. Figure 2 shows how this works. Mission context, prayer, and visioning are essential for every leader's development and team deployment, and every review of effectiveness and identification of key issues. From this central point of action, past experience is examined in the first part of the loop of circular causality, brought back to Spirit as mission context for prayer and visioning before future action is contemplated in the second part of the loop. This completes the mission context for prayer and visioning and initiates action.

Servant-empowering is another fractal pattern, proscriptive thinking operates at every level. People and teams are free to respond to their call of God, within the parameters of their mission focus and the core values of the church. Fractalled permission-giving happens in a climate of choice, personal affirmation, and trust. Leaders should look to deeper levels of leadership than holding office. At Prospect Road we have some leaders who have held high positions in the local church for decades. They have done and are doing good work but they need to be replaced to allow younger people to develop leadership gifts. Paul's Corinthian wisdom is helpful.

> "Now you are the body of Christ and individually members of it. And God has appointed in the church first apostles, second prophets, third teachers; then deeds of power, then gifts of healing, forms of assistance, forms of leadership, various kinds of tongues. Are all apostles? Are all prophets? Are all teachers? Do all work miracles? Do all possess gifts of healing? Do all speak in tongues? Do all interpret? But strive for the greater gifts. And I will show you a still more excellent way."
>
> (1 Cor. 12:28-31)

This is the only place where gifts are listed in a hierarchy, from the highest, (apostle) to the least (various kinds of tongues). Paul also exhorts us to "strive for the greater gifts"; so presumably all the gifts are attainable by any Christian and not something unique to an individual.

When the Uniting Church was formed in Australia, I was a pastor from the Congregational Church ministering in a Methodist Church. The Methodist Church had no previous history of Elders (which is typical of a Reformed type of polity), so I had the task of commissioning and training the first Elders in that particular church. To do so, I wrote my own training manual that included Paul's words on growing gifts. The new Elders and I set out to strive for the higher gifts. We avoided any controversy over tongues by interpreting the first level as "uninhibited witnessing" to our faith. We noted that "forms of leadership" can often be seen as the end point of Christian service, but they are only the second level. As Elders, we aspired to be "forms of assistance" or "helpers." As we learned and practiced, we experienced the dynamic of growth. First, we were hesitant and insecure in our role, then more practiced and assured. At the point when we were regularly experiencing ourselves as competent "helpers," God presented us with our first "healing" opportunity. Back to hesitancy and insecurity. The first "miracles" might have been around the corner when I was called to another church. However, I have a feeling that we reached the limit of most local church leaders. The higher gifts are for national and global ministry.

Now, at Prospect Road, this experience from way back can help our senior leaders. They will not be "retired" nor their experience lost in the mission formation of the church. We are encouraging them to grow the higher gifts of helpers and healers. I have a vision of a church where all the designated leaders are one- or two-year-old Christians, and there is a deep, rich vein of helpers and healers in the body of the church doing wonderful things for Jesus and backing and supporting the designated leaders by supporting and encouraging a rich community life. It, like other initiatives, will need prayer and vision sharing.

When something like a 7,000-strong New Hope Church is growing so fast, small church leaders and pastors feel at a loss about their own situation. Why go for a postmodern, proscriptive thinking, permission-giving network church when some observers, often at the center of a denomination, can point to a modernist, prescriptive thinking, authoritarian, line management church that seems to be doing so well?

We live in changing times. Some churches will do well in the old paradigm. Social class may be a factor. At Prospect Road Uniting Church in Adelaide, Australia, in an inner suburban cluster of churches in an area that is housing an increasing number of Gen-X professionals, the way we have chosen seems the best way forward to us. I wish I had meteoric growth to report, like New Hope, but I haven't. At the moment, we have a Red Queen effect—running hard to stay the same numbers—as our elderly originals move on. But we are not the same. There is life, energy, hope, and faith and ways in hand of using all this to grow and prosper. And that is light years ahead of where we were at the beginning.

---

[29] William Easum and Thomas Bandy, *Growing Spiritual Redwoods* (Nashville: Abingdon, 1997), p. 106ff. "The Spiritual Redwood signals a revolution in church organization."

[30] William Easum and Thomas Bandy, p. 123. "The inclination of the Spiritual Redwood is mutual trust, networks, and shared spiritual disciplines."

[31] "Simulating Self-Organising Innovation Networks (**SEIN**)." Final Conference, January 2001. http://www.uni-bielefeld.de/iwt/sein/

[32] Günter Küppers, *Self-organization: The Emergence of Order, From Local Interactions To Global Structures* (University of Bielefeld, July 1999).

[33] Günter Küppers, p. 11.

[34] See my discussion of Walsh in Chapter 2.

[35] Günter Küppers, p. 16. "Discursive negotiations serve as a coordinating mechanism for networks. This differs from formal contracts which dominate market coordination, as well as from the principle that instructions coordinate social interaction within hierarchical organizations."

[36] Thomas G. Bandy, *Christian Chaos: Revolutionizing the Congregation* (Nashville: Abingdon Press, 1999), p. 34.

[37] Thomas G. Bandy, Chapters 1, 2 and 3, especially p. 31ff. The diagram on p. 33 provides a helpful overview of this section of the book.

[38] Thomas G. Bandy, Chapter 5, especially p. 142ff.

[39] Günter Küppers, p. 18, including Figure 3.

[40] Günter Küppers, pp. 1, 12.

[41] Thomas G. Bandy, p. 36.

[42] William Easum, quoted from consultations and online coaching.

[43] Quoted by John Carroll in an interview on "ABC Radio National Religion Report" in Australia, on September 11, 2002. *The Fight Club* is a dis-

turbing movie, released in 1999. (See http://us.imdb.com/Title? 0137523). John Carroll is Reader in Sociology at Latrobe University in Melbourne, Australia. His book, *Humanism: The Wreck of Western Culture* (London: HarperCollins, 1993) provides more depth on this subject. He was being interviewed on the radio about his current book, *Terror: A Meditation on the Meaning of September11* (Melbourne: Scribe Publications, 2002).

[44] Judges 7: 4-7.

[45] Deuteronomy 34:1-9.

[46] Wayne Cordeiro. *Doing Church as a Team* (Ventura, CA: Regal Books, 2001), p. 179ff.

THINKING LOCAL IN A GLOBAL CONTEXT

A church leader can easily become so engrossed in the problems and issues that are on her or his doorstep that the global context that lies behind many of them is overlooked. If we do see beyond our own patch, then we may fail to see any connection between what we do locally and what happens across the globe. In this chapter we will consider the relationship of local mission and some of the global issues pressing on the local scene.

THE PLACE OF THE SACRED IN THE GLOBAL VILLAGE

When, years ago, the Russian cosmonaut quipped, "I can't see any sign of God up here!" he was not only expressing a scientific rationalist attitude towards religion but saying something rather more significant about a changing sense of the location of the sacred in the world. A new perspective has replaced the pre-modern, vertical orientation of the sacred. The view of Earth from outer space on the one hand has reinforced the objective, scientific rationalist view that nothing is subjective or sacred and on the other, has reinforced a spirituality that sees the blue planet as subjectively mysterious and spiritual. Both views pose problems for the local church. In the objective view, the local church is an irrelevant detail; in the subjective view the church can be a redundant, unnecessary sacred place in a world where everywhere is sacred.

Much of our church building in the past has been based on a view of the local village or the cathedral town. In that view, the church building marked the sacred place in that precinct: the place where, more than any other, people could experience a connection with God. Their lives and their faith were centered on God, and the village church with its spire or tower and vaulted ceilings symbolized the nature of that relationship. The spire on the horizon marked the sacred place and pointed upwards to indicate the vertical nature of the relationship with the divine.

When I visited Los Angeles for the first time my North American friends were quick to point out that Los Angeles is not America. Physically and possibly socially that's true. But Los Angeles epitomizes the emerging view of the global village. I experienced the urban landscape of Los Angeles as a kind of visual "no man's land," a blur of objectivity made up of passing concrete, cars, and constantly repeated urban development sameness, wrapped in a haze of photochemical smog. In among this landscape were homes, churches, shopping centers, and recreational venues, which were given meaning by being places of human subjectivity showing up in the blur like oases in a desert. When I came home to Adelaide, I observed the same thing—in somewhat less extreme form. In the global village, there are perhaps a dozen global landmarks: places that call forth a subjective response from the onlooker. The rest is part of the objective blur.

Louis Dupré, in his book, *Symbols of the Sacred*,[47] talks about the absence of subjectivity in modern art. "Great abstract art in painting, music and sculpture may provide the openness in which transcendence may be discovered; it does not show the transcendent itself."[48]

This openness allows the viewer to bring his or her own subjective view of transcendence to the art and for the art to contribute to the viewer's understanding and experience. Dupré goes on further to suggest that the non-subjectivity of modern art and its absence of transcendence can evoke a yearning for transcendence in the viewer. "Rarely do they obtain more than a sense of absence, a silence, or, at best, an inner space in which transcendence may become manifest again."[49]

Even when modern artists have completed commissioned

"sacred" works, the transcendent is not immediately apparent and requires "word" to understand and experience the sacred in them. "Here the religious ambiguity of modern art stands fully exposed, and with it the indispensability of language in all religious symbolism. Without the context or title, no one would be able to recognize those works as definitely religious."[50]

There is a correlation between Dupré's insights into the absence of transcendence in modern art and the absence of transcendence in a rationalist understanding of the global village. The absence creates an openness to the viewer's own subjectivity; the absence can evoke a longing for Spirit and the urban environment is given subjective meaning through naming and contextualization.

Openness is one of the values of the postmodern church that we espoused at the beginning of this book. The openness of Prospect Road resonates with the viewers' exploration of the non-specificity of the urban environment. When Spirit is absent from the worldview, people can explore their own spiritual yearnings and begin a quest for Spirit. The church is one place they may think to try. The Spirit relationships behind the open gates and greener pastures metaphor from Chapter 3 could provide opportunities to respond to feelings of spiritual need whenever an opportunity presents itself. Offering a range and choice of portals to Spirit gives the church a better chance of "being there" when the opportunity arises.

In the secular world of today, the first words and contexts that people apply to give subjective meaning to their world are unlikely to be "Church" or "Christian." The oases of meaning that they will create in the blur will be named "family," "work," "shopping," or "entertainment." Mission outreach will need to begin in those oases, and through relationships and especially a relationship with Jesus help people to name a "church" oasis of meaning in their lives. This relationship-building presence in those bits of the objective, rationalist world that have been allowed some subjectivity will increasingly be the only way that people find Christian faith and experience.

Our denominational planners' original plan for Prospect Road was that most of the centres would close and a nearby church, in a prominent position on a main road and in a regional shopping center, would become a regional church. But they were working from a Christendom worldview. They could not see that in a streetscape which is like an objective blur of cars, concrete, and suburbia, their prominent church is invisible; just another building with a porch, a place to stand and wait for the bus to the office or mall. Being a church set in a place given meaning by the word and context, "shopping" confers more challenges than advantages for mission outreach.

Ministry by walking about puts the symbolic leadership of the church in the key social nodes of the shopping precinct. Cell groups have the flexibility to grow organically in most of the oases of meaning. Establishing cell groups is the pressing "next step" for Prospect Road and, in hindsight, should have been implemented earlier.[51]

The alternative view of the global village—that it is a place with a spirituality that holds everything as sacred—also has problems for the church as sacred place. For, if everywhere is sacred or a locus for spirituality, why bother with church? How can the local church be seen as a particular sacred place or portal to God?

The Australian aboriginal people have a worldview in which all the land and its places are sacred, but some places are more significant than others. Bruce Chatwin, a popular author, uses the fiction genre to share his extensive interest and research into nomads. His book on the Australian aboriginal people, *The Songlines*,[52] describes the way these people relate local sacred places within an every-place-is-sacred worldview. Looking at the concept of songlines can give some helpful clues for local church mission outreach in this kind of context.

The songlines that Chatwin describes through the characters in his book are spiritual pathways across the continent of Australia that are traversed by knowing and sharing the song saga of the totemic spirit ancestors' journeys across the land.[53] Each aboriginal person becomes a custodian of part of the song and the pathway. Which song and which pathway is determined by the place where each person's mother first felt her or his quickening in her womb. The place is marked and its position on the closest songline noted. The baby is assigned the part of the songline that will be his or her responsibility. At boundaries between tribes, the songs of the next tribe's part of the songline is shared and learned, along with those of different totem groups and language groups. In theory, a person could traverse the continent, knowing the topography through the words of the song and hence staying on line. Each totemic spirit ancestor has its own songlines, so there is a matrix of pathways and songs from which position and journey can be accurately determined.

We no longer need songlines to navigate across the topography of the global village, but we do need to identify the transcendent places in our lives. One songline could link places of transforming spiritual experience. At the very least, they are the places where birth, death, and marriage are blessed and consecrated. Two of our senior members at Prospect Road are regular supporters of one of our more radically different outreach communities and worship services. They "blink" briefly whenever one of their long-remembered icons is moved or disposed of, but they keep coming. It is the spirituality of those life-phase blessings and not the furniture or the architecture that is the "place" that they cherish. At a previous church, a fashionable place to be married, a songline linking marriage, then often infant baptism and Spirit began to build a group of young parents in worship. Another path is a discipleship songline defined by the "topography" of spiritual experience that happens where significant spiritual transformation of people's lives is happening in a church. The witness of each person's changed life becomes another part of the song that helps them and other people to walk in the Way

The Australian aboriginal people exchange songs and ceremonies at gatherings and celebrations that are held at special places on the songline. Understanding life as a pilgrimage is a helpful way of integrating the experiences of significant places in life into a songline. For young people in particular, "nomadic" journeys seem to be a part of the search for meaning. At a time in their life that calls them to leave home but in a climate of great uncertainty about future "places," they turn to significant places in their national culture and global culture. Like pilgrimages of old, there is a spiritual quest there too, often barely recognized as being part of the experience but expressed in a sense of wonder and awe on arrival at the place. Young Australians are increasingly making pilgrimages to Gallipoli, the battlefield in Turkey where the Australian national character was founded, and journeys to the World War I killing fields of northern France, in search of identity and spirit. Taize and

Iona have become centres of pilgrimage for those people retaining some connection to the church, but for more and more it will be the secular centres where people find a sense of being part of a songline linking self, place, and Spirit.

New songline paths based on the four demographic, psychosocial, and character-defined communities we have at Prospect Road are beginning to emerge. An ideas-oriented small group resource—a "song" developed for the professional, do-it-yourself head "tribe" at Learnerlink, is the same "song, but with a different "language" when the group is from our lower status, relational, heart "tribe" study group. Similar lines are happening with the alternative lifestyle, sensory, gut spirituality "sung" with a different language in the Parent/Child strand at Parentlink. This kind of songline is beginning to extend beyond the Prospect Road outreach communities with our "companion planting" relationships and may extend later to similar groupings in other denominations. In the future, songlines traced in this way will be more sought out than the formal ties linking congregations through denominational structures.

It is my hope that this book will be a "place of spiritual quickening" for small churches around the globe that will induct each church into a songline where each has a part of the song to sing and a part of the Way for which they accept responsibility and which is "sung" and shared in celebration events across the globe. The EasumBandy Community's online forums have identified for me a number of soul brothers and sisters who sing the same song and walk a different section of the same path.

Too many churches are still living out of the Christendom village church model of spirituality and expecting the church to be honored as the sacred place at the center of the village. In the global village, there is no central place. We are in a pre-Christian mission field where any person expressing spiritual yearning is offered a relationship with Jesus as an option and where the Christian walk of believers is blessed and encouraged.

Globalization and effective local action

Australia is a big country, and when one's family is scattered over the eastern half of it, a lot of long-distance driving is needed to make family visits. Sometimes, to make the journey more interesting and to avoid big trucks, I would take secondary roads. As I went through the little towns on the way, I would play a kind of "survivor" game with them. Which ones would decline and which ones would thrive? I would note things like the look of the town. Towns that are in decline have a look of despair about them. Empty shops on Main Street, deferred maintenance on buildings, low stock levels in shops, and tired and dispirited service. Towns that are thriving have a look of hope about them. There are entrepreneurial businesses on Main Street, an investment in the future, and good customer care. Somewhere in that town there is an innovative person or group that has decided to turn the town's fortunes around.

The same influences are at work in the local neighborhoods of our major cities. Large shopping malls are putting the old "mom and dad" local stores out of business and their empty shop fronts have, in turn, depressed the appearance and tone of what was once the bustling heart of the local area. The trend of closing local bank branches and other services in favor of regional centres has added to this. The phenomenon of moving services to somewhere that provides greater opportunity to increase profit is not simply a local occurrence but a trend that depresses regions and even nations when applied on a global scale. This is the shadow side of globalization.

Don Edgar in *The Patchwork Nation: Rethinking Government, Rebuilding Community*,"[54] discusses the implications of globalization. Edgar, previously the Director of the Institute of Family Studies, a respected research organization in Australia, comments on these changes and their importance. Edgar believes that people's sense of cultural identity is formed at the local level. When the place that is the crucible of this cultural identity disappears or is debased, then new foci for cultural identity are sought. Globalization, as an outcome of modern, economic rationalism is putting the work, family, and local community bases of cultural identity at risk. Edgar says,

> We seem to face two opposing forces; globalization and convergence on the hand, versus fragmentation and localization, on the other. Nations are forced together via technology and economic

forces, yet nations are internally split by ethnic, religious, and political conflict, as various interests struggle to preserve their own sense of identity.[55]

Edgar describes globalization and the need for local cultural identity as opposing forces. It might be better to view their apparent polarity as a paradox. Clearly, the market forces driving globalization are here to stay. Cultural identity is a necessary reality too, but we need to encourage more peaceful ways of finding cultural identity than reactive opposition.

Edgar proposes that local community can be rebuilt through broad networks of participation involving local families, businesses, and government agencies in implementing important services. Edgar sees nations, and ultimately the globe, as being a stitching together of culture-defining local places. However, his proposals for doing this all involve government bureaucratic involvement, and as we have seen from circular causality, networks do not work like that. Giving local people a role in deciding their own future needs someone or some group at the local level to initiate an action-reflection process. It will not happen from the top down, or initially, from a bottom-up democratic consensus.

There is a small town in rural Australia, not far from the regional centre where my son lives. It is a place he takes us when we visit as a good destination for a Sunday afternoon drive. The town, originally a small service centre for the surrounding farms, has reinvented itself. A small street of "companion plantings" of specialty shops selling coffee and cake, "home-made and country fresh" preserves and produce, antiques, craft work, an art gallery, and other similar shops support the original country post office store to cater for four distinct customer communities. There are the day-trippers like we were, those making a comfort stop on their journey out of the state capital, tourists to the region and the residual farmers, retaining their service center because of the increased turnover at the store. The place is now abuzz, especially on weekends. Someone local looked at the demographics, psychosocial groupings, and character and countervailed against the economic rationalism that would have consigned this place to history. Now the place in which many generations found identity will continue to nurture their being and that of many more generations to come. The towns I assessed as survivors on my travels all have a similar innovative drive, each presenting its own unique solution to economic rationalist, globalization pressures.

Initiatives and innovation that change towns and neighborhoods use similar methods to those that this book suggests will transform small churches. The public can learn how to take effective action for its future from the example of local church transformation. When, at the beginning of the changes we made to the church, some centres ceased worship for a while, rumors swept the district that we were closing the churches. People were relieved when they found out that the church was staying in the area, even though they did not attend and had no intention of attending. The church was part of the "business" of the "patch." If it went, its presence would be missed and the quality of the neighborhood diminished. A transformed church, relevant to its mission field, encourages local business to be relevant to its local market. The church/mission field, business/market, and local/global become different parts of a fractal pattern. In practice then, Edgar's patchwork will become less and less like a quilt and more and more like a swirling, computer-generated fractal pattern.

Visualizing the patchwork as a fractal pattern helps remind us that there is no linear, cause and effect relationship between local action and global power, which is just as well. In a line management model of the globe, the difference in power between those at the top and those at the bottom is overwhelming. Adelaide is a major center for automobile manufacturing. A while ago, one of the local plants was under threat of closure. This would have been disastrous for our local economy. Our government made representations to the global company concerned. Its chairman politely made it clear that it was his management team that would make the decision, not the state. When our most powerful people are powerless, where are we?

Fortunately, global influences have more to do with chaos theory than line management. If, as it has been said, "A butterfly flapping its wings in the Amazon jungle can generate a typhoon on the other side of the world," then local action can have a larger effect than is apparent in the local time and place. In particular, Spirit-inspired men and women have changed the course of history, as we noted earlier, and the Bible is full of stories of ordinary people with God-given vision and purpose affecting the power structures of their day.

In the scientific rationalist world in which we live, spiritual experiences are strange and a little disquieting. However, they can be powerfully motivating and lead to very practical outcomes. They infuse ministry concerns with the power of God and become triggers for circular causality and innovation networks. Paradoxically, the greater openness of our times also makes it easier to talk about such things.

About thirty years ago, I was sitting in the front room of my house, watching the news report of the state funeral of a prominent Australian political elder statesman when a voice spoke to me. It said two things, "The last verse of the book of Jonah," and, "I have given you a city." It was strange, to say the least! Jonah is not a biblical text I know intimately, so I immediately found a Bible to look it up. This is what was written.

> And should I not be concerned about Nineveh, that great city, in which there are more than a hundred and twenty thousand persons who do not know their right hand from their left, and also many animals? (Jonah 4:11)

I took both statements to be a word from God to me, but I kept them to myself. In my tradition in those days such things were not supposed to happen. But from then on, I kept looking beyond my immediate patch to the city that was promised. A number of times since, I have thought, "This is it! This is the city that God promised," but nothing has matched so far. But it has been a powerful motivating vision, which along with my "call" story has kept me focused outward to a larger mission field and towards those in "Nineveh" for whom God is concerned. Reflecting on it now, I see many parallels in my life to the story of Jonah. It has become a story that grounds my life story in God's purpose for me.

Motivating visions like this that are directly given by God are a reminder of our connection to God's strong and countervailing but loving influence to the principalities and powers of the world.[56] Motivating visions are what give individuals the courage to initiate change and the confidence to discern the Spirit of God in the processes of change.

Discerning God's spirit is crucial to innovation networks. When the mission context is taken to God in prayer a vision for action evolves that colors the development of leadership and the formation of teams to effect the changes. The individual motivating vision is the outcome of the personal Spirit point in circular causality. Then, in a larger fractal pattern, the individual sense of action arising from personal vision works at the Spirit point in circular causality for a group to pray, vision, recruit, do, and reflect to get innovative action under way.

Just as my "Nineveh" motivating story grounds my life and mission in God's purpose for me, so motivating stories ground the life and mission of the church at each level of mission engagement, from the personal to the global. Included within this fractal layering are biblical stories,[57] which when incorporated with other motivating stories "sponsor" motivating visions for the outreach community and congregation to initiate circular causality and innovative mission engagement. Thus Spirit influences the context, the prayer, and the visioning in every layer, in an organic way. This is not line management but a relationship of God, person, team, and task that makes use of the power and influence of God in the situation. And over and beyond these stories is the New Testament story—beginning with revelations to Mary and Joseph, the shepherds and the wise men and working in a circular causality loop through the life of Jesus and the calling of the disciples to the cross and resurrection, then through the work and ministry of the early church to a new cycle beginning with Revelation. God's power and human faithfulness combine at every level to give people the courage to take initiative in mission in the face of principalities and powers. Thus at every fractal level, the power of God guides and influences the process and ultimately changes the world.

Earlier, in the quotation from Edgar, we were reminded of another response to globalization. Like the missionary church of our time, issue-based "action" groups use innovation networks and work out of circular causality, but anger, not faith, gives them the spirit and courage to face uncertainty. In some instances, it is not too strong to say that hatred or rage drives them. These strong emotions can block a more comprehensive and inclusive view of the situation. In deciding how to respond to the principalities and powers of globalization, the choice asked at the trial of Jesus becomes contemporary. Barabbas or Jesus? The choice is between demonstrations and renewal, violence and peace. The crowd chose Barabbas and as a consequence, Jerusalem was destroyed. New believers chose Jesus and the world was changed. Instead of hatred and opposition the Church offered love.

The first church engaged with the world in response to Christ's command in Luke 24:47-49:

> Repentance and forgiveness of sins is to be proclaimed in his name to all nations, beginning from Jerusalem. You are witnesses of these things. And see, I am sending upon you what my Father promised; so stay here in the city until you have been clothed with power from on high.

They went with the power of the Spirit of God to offer a way to exercise effective local action to people who felt powerless. They did not impose their power on the different cultures they faced as they went out in obedience to Christ. Love adapted to flourish within each new culture. Starting in Jerusalem, they first went with love and compassion to those living with Greek culture and language and overcame the liberal/conservative divide. Then love touched an Ethiopian eunuch, and they overcame the race and sexuality divide. Then they went to the Samaritans and overcame the divide of ancient prejudices. Finally, love was brought to the Romans and the Gentiles, and the separation from the principalities and powers was overcome. Each new encounter would have been a challenge to their Jewish identity, and they wrestled with the tendency to impose that identity on others but were led by the Spirit to instead nurture an indigenous Christian identity with every culture that they met. It all started with a small church in Jerusalem that went out to tackle the globalization of its time with the power of the Spirit of Jesus.

The local church that becomes a church at large has a similar adaptability and openness. It reaches out to its mission field with the intention of bringing the good news of Jesus so that it is indigenous to that culture. Change then grows from within rather than being imposed. As the colonial influences of modernism wane in the third world, the great commission is finding fulfillment in indigenous churches expressing the good news strongly and effectively out of the local culture. Third-world churches are the fastest growing in the world. Churches like Prospect Road that are open and at large will build similar cultural identity beyond the economic and social consequences of globalization, stepping out of marketplace competition to recognize "Christ-likeness" in different cultural expressions of it and without any need to harmonize the differences.

Finally, different gifts are needed for people to operate with Spirit on the broadest mission field. In New Testament times, the Christians who took Spirit initiatives at the world level were the apostles. Their apostleship was not determined by the management gifts, moneymaking entrepreneurial gifts, gifts in medicine or science, or artistic and creative gifts, even though these gifts could have been very helpful. Instead, apostleship was determined by those with the "higher spiritual gifts" of 1 Corinthians 12:27-31.

As the disciples' spheres of action extended higher, broader, and deeper into the culture, so the higher gifts of helper, healer, miracle worker, teacher, and prophet have a greater importance. It is a higher gift to heal and conciliate in a polarized situation than to demonstrate. It is a higher gift to bring about a peaceful, transformation miracle than to change culture through violence. It is a higher gift to teach a different understanding than the tit-for-tat cycles of injustice and retribution that sear and divide people, sometimes for hundreds of years. It is a higher gift to vision a future that includes all people in its blessings. That is why it is important for the church to nurture the higher gifts beyond the sticking point of "administration," the second to lowest of the gifts in Paul's Corinthian list. Christians are called to seek the higher gifts. When higher gifts get stitched into the fabric of the local situation, the world will change.

During a time of crisis counseling, I telephoned my colleague, Peter Kahrimanis, for prayer, partly because he has a gift for prayer and partly because the issue for which I needed prayer was one where I knew he had some experience. We prayed for a situation compounded by abuse, separation, drugs, and petty crime. Peter's prayer opened my eyes to a new way of dealing with the seemingly impossible. Slowly, carefully, and with power, he named caring love, reunion, release from addiction, and a return to good living for the person for whom we prayed. Now my task was "infilling" God's will in the situation rather than wondering what on earth to do or where to begin.

What could be done with five, small, elderly, declining congregations? If, like Peter's prayer, we see lively communities crowded with people of all ages we will respond differently. Like assembling a complex jigsaw puzzle with a badly damaged box cover, we look at all the bits and pieces of opportunity that present themselves in our ministry and try to work out how God's purpose can be achieved. We manage to fit together a few pieces in one corner, some more in the middle, and others at the base. In time, with perseverance and holding the vision, more and more areas of the puzzle are filled. People come, look and find a piece or two that have been missed, and add them in until the completion of the picture is inevitable. That's the point we are at with Prospect Road.

Christianity operates in the same way. It works from the big picture of the kingdom of God being "at hand." The kingdom of God is a sanctification of all life, which is, paradoxically, still to come but already present. We live, as Dietrich Bonhoeffer wrote, in the "penultimate" time but influenced by the ultimate. Discerning the kingdom is to discern Jesus in our life and relationships, leading us towards establishing the kingdom and at the same time blessing us to be the kingdom. Like the jigsaw metaphor, we need to discern the pieces of the kingdom that will, when all are put in place, complete the picture. However this is still a mechanistic, "modern" metaphor. It is better to use the organic metaphors Jesus used for being and becoming the kingdom of God: seed, yeast, and birth. When Jesus proclaimed, "the kingdom of God is at hand," he was inviting us to see the seed, the yeast, and the pregnant body and envisage the tree, the loaf, and the baby that these things portend.

Perhaps your church would be like the seed beginning to sprout, the dough beginning to rise, the pregnancy beginning to show—enough that we can lay claim to the plant, the bread, and the baby. We invite you to be a part of our harvest, our feast, and our thanksgiving.

---

[47] Louis Dupré, *Symbols Of the Sacred* (Grand Rapids: Eerdmans, 2000), p. 87ff.

[48] Dupré, p. 87.

[49] Dupré, p. 88.

[50] Dupré, p. 89.

[51] Thomas Bandy, *Christian Chaos*. The second major section of this book, "Turning the Laity Loose: Organizational Change Through Cell Groups and Mission Teams," p. 179ff., provides comprehensive material for transitioning and transitioned churches that will be customized for Prospect Road.

[52] Bruce Chatwin, *The Songlines* (Jonathan Cape, 1987; my edition by London: Picador/Pan Books, 1988).

[53] Chatwin, p. 61ff.

[54] Don Edgar, *The Patchwork Nation*.

[55] Edgar, p. 83.

[56] Walter Wink, *Engaging the Powers*. Wink gives a very comprehensive coverage to this subject in the whole book, but his reference in Chapter 14 to loving enemies is a useful focus here.

[57] Thomas Bandy, *Kicking Habits (Upgrade Edition): Welcome Relief For Addicted Churches* (Nashville: Abingdon, 2001). From p. 242ff., Bandy lists five biblical theological motifs that would be a useful beginning point for churches trying to identify their motivating story.

Notes

108710